Tough Plants in a Fragile Land

Saving Our Planet, One Garden at a Time

Tough Plants in a Fragile Land

Saving Our Planet, One Garden at a Time

by

Fritzie von Jessen

DORRANCE PUBLISHING CO., INC.
PITTSBURGH, PENNSYLVANIA 15222

The contents of this work including, but not limited to, the accuracy of events, people, and places depicted; opinions expressed; permission to use previously published materials included; and any advice given or actions advocated are solely the responsibility of the author, who assumes all liability for said work and indemnifies the publisher against any claims stemming from publication of the work.

First Printing

For more information or to order additional books, please contact:
Dorrance Publishing Co., Inc.
701 Smithfield Street
Third Floor
Pittsburgh, Pennsylvania 15222
U.S.A.

1-800-788-7654
www.dorrancebookstore.com

For Tanya and Tim,
with boundless love and constant admiration.

"Life began in a garden"

Contents

"In all things of nature there is something marvelous." —Aristotle

Foreword

2006 was a year without spring. Then, a prolonged summer with record breaking heat was followed almost immediately with record cold—in some places freezing—temperatures. Climate change or global warming? It's very possible we'll have more years like that.

This led me to research plants native to the Colorado Desert, their use in the planned landscapes, and their benefits to the ecosystem. I found it fascinating to note how well native plants weathered these extremes which caused devastation among exotics (non-natives). Captivated by my discoveries, I felt compelled to share what I had learned.

Over the years I have developed a passionate love affair with the desert. I have a burning desire to share with you my discoveries of all the wonderful qualities of native plants and the sensual joys of gardening with nature in this wonderful place, the Colorado Desert. And this is what this book is all about.

Through these pages I'm inviting you to tour and explore with me the magic of the desert. It's my hope that you, too, will be seduced by the plants and wildlife that inhabit the desert landscape where shadows are strong and vivid. It's my wish that you'll perpetuate the desert look in your own garden.

Although the focus of this book is the Colorado Desert, its plants and its wildlife, the principles can be applied to all regions. I hope this book will help to show how an individual can contribute to healing our ailing planet—and have fun doing so.

Introduction

Nobody is born with a green thumb. Some might get an early exposure to gardening through the influence of parents or grandparents with a keen interest in growing things. I wasn't one of those. I'm a city girl. My parents and my grandmother played cards and smoked cigars. Smoke-filled rooms and loud voices were my natural habitat. I grew up in Copenhagen, Denmark, and my exposure to nature was limited to a couple of weeks at the beach where my family rented a cabin during the summer. What I remember most from these carefree childhood days is gorging on some kind of berries that grew wild on a heath-like strip of land separating the cluster of cabins from the beach. To this day, I don't know what those berries were but obviously they did me no harm.

As a young woman, I moved to New York City. I had stepped from smoky rooms into streets where the soot in the air brought tears to my eyes. My horticultural knowledge was scant. I knew the difference between a rose and a dandelion: you couldn't buy dandelions at the florists'.

Then I got married and my husband transplanted me to a house on Long Island with more than an acre of land—mostly lawn with a lot of dandelions and a few rose bushes. For our first anniversary he gave me a lawnmower! My outdoor experiences were about to begin.

I would push this ugly, unwieldy mower over what seemed to be miles of grass. Imagine the continuous cycle of watering and fertilizing to make the grass grow, then spending hours and energy to keep it short. It was, I think, the beginning of my love-hate relationship with gardening. I loved the look of a well-manicured, weed free lawn, but hated all the work involved.

I began adding flowers, became a budding gardener, so to speak. At first, I planted annuals for instant gratification. Now I was dead-heading (removing spent flowers) to keep them blooming all summer, only to have to pull them out with the onset of cold weather, and then start all over in spring.

Next, I discovered perennials. Now I had the fun of creating and enjoying an ever-changing landscape. I became a gardener.

Seesawing between the joys and the frustrations of parenthood, I found equilibrium in my garden. I dug and I cut; I weeded and I planted. I watched things grow. Then, in a blink of an eye, I had an empty nest—the kids were in college and my husband and I had separated. It was time to move on.

I made a trip to California to visit with friends. Arriving in Palm Springs, my first impression was of the air: how clean and light it was; how easy to breathe. I could feel my lungs expanding. The next couple of weeks I drove around, exploring. Before I left, I had decided. This was a place I would spend the rest of my life.

I had found a house with a garden that reminded me of my garden on Long Island: an extensive lawn, colorful petunias, a few palm trees, and, instead of privet hedges, it had tall oleanders for a privacy screen. It'd be an easy transition. Or so I thought. That was more than twenty years ago.

The beauty of the desert is subtle. It doesn't slap you in the face as do more traditional and flamboyant landscapes. It reveals itself slowly like the bud of a cactus flower unfolding. After disclosing its unique magnificence, it grabs you like the catclaw acacia. Living things in the desert are invisible from a distance; the desert must be viewed up close. The pale, mysterious wilderness of the desert both threatens and enthralls. Away from houses and development, one is surrounded by a silence disturbed only by breezes rustling Mormon tea and desert sage and the chatter of water bubbling to the surface from underground springs. Within a short time I was hooked.

Ravens belong wholeheartedly to the desert

I now call the desert home. It's the place where a clear sky the color of faded denim arcs the valley floor. I watch as shreds of vapor tease with the promise of rain until air currents carry them away—a promise unfulfilled.

Mountains, polished through centuries with desert varnish, loom like sentinels guarding the fragile land. I am in awe at the spectacle of dawn gilding their bulk in a fiery glow. I observe the sun starting its daily journey and I see a chuckwalla skittering from its nightly shelter to absorb the warmth atop one of the many rocks and boulders strewn across the landscape. California ground squirrels scurry across the sand. Then, when the sun reaches its zenith, the desert rests. Only a whisper of wind breaks the silence of the midday desert, calling attention to its wild loneliness and spiritual solitude.

As shadows stretch, twilight folds the mountains in soft purple gauze. It spreads a painter's palette of pastels, rose and gold, peach and turquoise, across the sky before giving way to a star filled night.

When stars prick the indigo canopy and the moon draws eerie silhouettes, the desert comes alive. The white underbelly of a barn owl is visible as this large raptor ghosts across the heavens. The lonely cry of a coyote and the trill of the mockingbird puncture the silence. Plants release their fragrance to perfume the night air. Sacred Datura blossoms like delicate porcelain cups glow in the moonlight. An occasional rain liberates the pungent scent of creosote bushes; the smell of the desert.

Angel's trumpet, Jimson weeds Sacred Datura (*Datura wrightii*)

The haunting beauty of the desert captivates the spirit and nourishes the soul. It is a sad paradox that as more people become attuned to this strange beauty and relocate to the desert, more of the desert is being lost to development. Under the frown of the mountains, bulldozers raze the indigenous life to build accommodations for the newcomers who, being unfamiliar with the land, unwittingly destroy the very characteristics that attracted them here.

It becomes imperative for the individual homeowner and gardener to preserve the unique character of the desert by cultivating native vegetation and become guardians of the land. Our responsibility for a better environment begins in our garden; by selecting the proper plants we can reduce the green waste that go into landfills, the chemicals that poison the soil, and the fumes that pollute the air.

The garden becomes an expression of our creativity. We can shape our immediate environment in a way that pleases our senses and sustains desert life.

Choosing the road to gardening with nature is most often the path of least resistance. Less maintenance is needed which leaves you more time to enjoy your surroundings.

Dragonfly

Long ago I bid farewell to lawn and petunias. Most of my oleanders perished due to mysterious disease and had to be removed. This provided a marvelous opportunity to replace these exotics with more desert appropriate plants. Once the lawn was gone, my garden became dazzlingly alive. When chemicals no longer poisoned the soil the bugs began to thrive. Insects and bugs attracted birds galore as well as many kinds of lizards which, in turn, attracted small mammals. Rather than trying to subjugate nature I have created a working partnership with the natural world. Native plants can fulfill both aesthetic and functional needs and require little attention since they are well adapted to climate and soil.

Blue Dasher

In the mornings, I step outside to see orange and blue dragonflies hovering over the swimming pool like tiny helicopters. Mourning doves congregate around the birdfeeder, gracefully making room for finches and white-crowned sparrows. It's like waking up with a lover; a tug of happiness suffuses my whole being and I embrace the coming day with a sense of wonder.

Let me serve as your guide in selecting plants for your garden, a roadmap to spark your own creativity in fashioning a sustainable environment in your back yard. Let me nurture your wish to do something practical about maintaining our disappearing habitat so that you, too, will feel my joy along the way. I'll admit to what I did wrong—planting agaves with very unfriendly thorns next to my entrance. It's my hope you'll reap the benefit of my costly mistakes; most of which had to do with not allowing for the mature size of a plant.

A dear friend of mine thumbed through a garden book. "Not enough pictures," she said with dismay and put the book back on its shelf. Photographs stimulate and provide ideas so I've included plenty of those. After all, I can rhapsodize over a desert marigold: it's a small perennial that reseeds easily; it has pretty, yellow, daisy-like flowers and blooms year round. Do you visualize a dandelion?

Desert marigold (*Baileya multiradiata*) in front of blue salvia

"One touch of nature makes us all kin." —Shakespeare

Where Is the Colorado Desert?

When I mention the Colorado Desert, many of my fellow desert dwellers get a blank look on their face. "Duh! This is California, not Colorado."

The Colorado Desert was named by geologist William Phipps Blake of the 1853 U.S. Pacific Railroad Survey before the state of Colorado received its name. The desert, he observed, owed its origin to the Colorado River by the deposition of sediment and displacement of seawater.

California's Colorado Desert is a part of the larger Sonoran Desert, which extends across southwest North America. The Colorado Desert reaches from the Mexican border in the south to the higher elevation Mojave Desert in the north and from the Colorado River in the east to the Peninsular Mountain range in the west. Although the highest peaks of the Peninsular Range reach elevations of 10,834 feet, the majority of the Colorado Desert lies at a relatively low elevation, less than 1,000 feet, with the lowest point of the desert floor at 275 feet below sea level in the Salton Trough. Most of the region's mountains do not exceed 3,000 feet. These ranges block moist coastal air and rain, producing an arid climate.

However, lest you underestimate the dignity of these mountains, I want to point out that Mt. San Jacinto is the steepest mountain in North America, rising vertically over 10,000 feet from the valley floor and going through five climatic zones. Mt. San Gorgonio of the Transverse Range is the highest mountain in Southern California at 11,502 feet.

The Colorado Desert's climate distinguishes it from other deserts. The area experiences greater summer daytime temperatures and almost never suffers frost. In addition, the Colorado Desert, especially toward the southern portion of the region, has two rainy seasons per year, in the winter and late summer. However, the rainy season might consist of just a few drops of water and increased humidity, not the monsoons which is characteristic of the greater Sonoran Desert. The rain tends to be localized. I have seen rain falling on one side of my house and not on the other side. And my house is not very big. The Colorado Desert is among the driest of the North American deserts.

Some areas of the Colorado Desert have undergone significant growth in recent decades. As a result they face challenges to regional wildlife; many species of which are unique to the Colorado Desert.

Coachella Valley is home to a series of fast-growing communities stretching from Palm Springs eastward to Indio and including outlying communities of Mecca, Coachella, Thermal, and North Shore in the southeast. Some consider this progress, but I am saddened by the loss of native habitats. Population in the valley's nine cities and surrounding unincorporated area is projected to increase from approximately 330,000 in 2000 to between 475,000 and 518,000 residents in 2020.

Growth is also noteworthy in southern Imperial County, near the border cities of El Centro and Calexico on the US-Mexico border. Conversion of agricultural fields to residential development presents a major threat to wildlife.

In the Colorado Desert region, non-native plants have become invasive. These species tend to spread from adjacent developments and threaten the survival of native species. In addition, exotics attract wildlife non-native to the area which further leads to the decline of native species. Brown-headed cowbirds thrive in many human altered habitats. They lay their eggs in flycatcher nests, forcing flycatcher parents to depart their nest or raise the cowbird young at the expense of their own.

Although federal and state wildlife agencies and non-governmental agencies have stepped in to promote conservation, that's not enough. As individual homeowners and gardeners, we can help by being aware and conscientious in our choice of plant material for the garden.

Maybe you believe that your small garden is not going to make a difference to the environment. One grain of sand does not make a beach (or a desert). However, a multitude of smaller lots will make a difference. Each garden is individual and reflects the homeowner's taste but you can create a regional identity. I got together with my neighbors to coordinate the landscape in front of our properties for a unified look using native plants. We each had our favorites so each frontage is unique. My next-door neighbor's house is ultra modern (but green: solar energy et al). He chose spiky, sculptural plants such as agaves and cacti. My preference was low maintenance but with a softer more lush look. I had plenty of native plants to choose from. Think about starting a grassroots movement in your neighborhood.

Who Was First?

The Colorado Desert is rich in history. It has been inhabited by Native Americans for more than 10,000 years. Along the Colorado River the Mojave and Yuma farmed their corn, beans, pumpkins, and melons in seasonal washes. Further north, the Chimehuevi hunted small game around the Providence Mountains.

Coachella Valley was once part of a vast inland sea and tiny, fossilized mollusk shells can be found in just about every remote area. It is believed it got its name from the Spanish word for seashell "Conchella."

The first people to settle in Coachella Valley were the Cahuilla Indians. More than 3,000 years ago the Cahuilla people settled in Palm Springs around the area's natural hot springs. During the heat of the summer months they would escape into the relative coolness of Tahquitz Canyon, where relics of their occupancy can still be found. They were hunters and gatherers and had a special relationship to the land. The creosote bush was their drugstore; the mesquite tree was their supermarket.

The Europeans came next. In the mid-1800s camels were used to survey the area. Starting in the 1840s prospectors with pack mules or burros sought their riches in the Colorado Desert. Gold, silver, and copper in large quantities were found within its borders and mines were established. Later, when the Southern Pacific Railroad opened their route through here, followed by the discovery of abundant artesian wells later in the 19th century, the area began to expand.

Date garden in Indio

Thermal, Mecca, Coachella, and Indio saw the birth of the date industry on a commercial basis in the early 1900s.

In the early 1900s Palm Springs was known chiefly as a health resort, primarily for tubercular patients. However, it didn't take long before it began to attract visitors who came to enjoy the warm sunshine, the pure, dry air, and the quiet of this restful desert retreat.

Since the 1930s, when Bing Crosby, Charles Farrell, and Ralph Bellamy founded the area's first tennis club in Palm Springs, the area has been a magnet for Hollywood stars. It became a playground for the rich and famous.

An influx of retirees, senior citizens, and winter residents were soon to follow. The Coachella Valley was a safe haven for hay fever allergy sufferers. That was before the surge of golf courses and year-round lawns. As I write this, there are 136 golf courses in Coachella Valley and the construction of more are in the planning.

In the 1980s and 1990s the Coachella Valley became a major real estate destination. Lower housing cost and apartment rents attracted families with children and young adults. The tourist attraction we know as Palm Springs has been exported worldwide, resulting in an increase of international visitors.

In the Imperial Valley, Spanish explorer Melchior Diaz was one of the first Europeans to visit in 1540. Here the economy is heavily based on agriculture due to the availability of irrigation water, which is supplied wholly from the Colorado River via the All-American Canal. Imported water and a long growing season allow two crop cycles each year and makes the Imperial Valley a major source of winter fruits and vegetables, cotton, and grain for U.S. and international markets. Alfalfa is another major crop produced in the Imperial Valley.

Over the years the Imperial Valley region has become a tourist destination. Many visitors come to the area to visit the Salton Sea, California's largest inland lake. The Salton Sea is 35 miles long and up to 15 miles wide with an average depth of 20 feet. It was formed by accident around 1905 when a cut was made in the banks of the Colorado River to irrigate the Imperial Valley. Flood waters broke through the cut, causing the river to flow north into the Salton Sink, an ancient sea bed. The lake's surface is 228 feet below sea level with no outlet.

Salton Sea

Bird watching is rewarding at this body of salt water where more than 400 species of migratory birds visit between October and May.

Wetlands by Salton Sea

Blue heron and egrets have been spotted at or near the lake.

Another unique feature is the New River. This flows from south to north from the nearby border town Mexicali. The creation of the New River started in the autumn of 1904, when heavy rainfall and snowmelt caused the Colorado River to swell and breach an Imperial Valley dike. The New River gave birth to the Salton Sea.

The Algodones Dunes were formerly named Sand Hills. They are formed by windblown beach sand from ancient Lake Cahuilla. Some sand crests reach a height of more than 300 feet. Rare plants, such as the endangered species of Coachella Valley milk vetch, are only found on sand dunes.

As recently as fifty years ago sand dunes covered most of Coachella Valley. Now only five percent of these dunes are left—at the Coachella Valley Preserve where several species of endangered animals can be found. The Coachella Valley fringe-toed lizard and the flat-tailed horned lizard are two of these rare animals. Coachella Valley giant sand-threader crickets and sidewinders can also be seen in the dunes. Desert kangaroo rats like the soft sand for their burrows.

The harvester ant is on the bottom of the food chain and important for the survival of the fringe-toed lizard and for the flat-tailed horned lizard.

Fringe-toed lizard

What Is a Desert?

Big horn sheep. Photo by Loretta Currie

Webster's dictionary defines desert as:

A dry barren, often sandy region that can naturally support little or no vegetation. 2. A wild uncultivated and uninhabited region. 3. An area devoid of character or quality: Wasteland.

I respectfully disagree, Mr. Webster.

Heavy winter rains are followed by a phenomenal outburst of bloom which transforms the land into a vast flower garden of sand verbena, primroses, lupines, and other wildflowers. Okay, so it doesn't rain every year, but the seeds are there, dormant, waiting, and, when the rains do come, a spectacular display of flowers dazzles the eyes.

The desert an uninhabited region? I don't think so. The desert is home to bighorn sheep, coyotes, mountain lions and bobcats, rattlesnakes, desert tortoises, and turkey vultures. All manner of rodents and insects flourish in this parched land.

Thousands of species of wildlife and plants have adapted to the arid climate and all are interdependent on one another. Some are prey; some are predators. Some are pollinators; some are propagators. Insects feed on plants. Lizards consider insects a tasty morsel. Snakes keep the rodent population under control. The desert tortoise is an herbivore that feeds on herbs, grasses, and wildflowers. It's able to live where ground temperature may exceed 140 degrees Fahrenheit. It spends 95 percent of its life in underground burrows and it can survive for a year or more without access to water.

Desert tortoise. Photo www.desertusa.com

Tiny Costa's hummingbirds flit among desert flowers to feed on their nectar. Insects and spiders are part of their diet as well.

Costa's hummingbird

Insects and bugs thrive in the hot, dry climate; each has its own purpose. Although the bite of a black widow spider can be deadly, or at the very least cause a bad reaction, (I recommend wearing gloves when gardening) the silken thread of its web provides a strong, elastic material for the hummingbird to build its nest. Bees of many species are useful pollinators and their honey is a wonderful food source.

Bee pollinating cactus flower

Even inanimate objects, such as rocks, have a role to play. Their surface quickly absorbs the sun's heat to provide a warming plate for cold-blooded creatures. The cracks between boulders are a safe haven for small animals to hide from predators, such as a red-tailed hawk swooping to snatch an unsuspecting deer mouse or a kangaroo rat with its powerful talons.

Burrowing owls find refuge underground; great horned owls and screech owls all thrive in their desert habitat.

The roadrunner is a bird with an attitude. She struts across the valley floor, kicking up dirt to dislodge a potential meal of insects, lizards, or maybe a rattlesnake.

Verdin

The sprightly verdin is a desert bird only slightly larger than a hummingbird. A ray of sun illuminates her yellow head above dull gray plumage and chestnut shoulder patches. She builds her nest, a globular mass of thorny twigs lined with feathers, hidden among the barbed branches of desert shrubs. Gambel's quail scuttles in the brush scratching for insects.

Gambel's quail

From the top of a mesquite tree a phaenopepla surveys his domain. His crested head and dapper body sculpts a black shape outlined against soft lucid blue.

Phaenopepla. Photo by David Schwaegler

The packrat builds its midden and guards the entrance with spiny joints of cholla cactus. As the next generation builds atop the existing abode, a midden can reach a height of many feet.

Nervous bunny rabbits and jackrabbits find refuge in the thicket of a creosote bush, hiding from their many predators. Ground squirrels and deer mouse coexist with mule deer and bighorn sheep. The Coachella Valley fringe-toed lizard is unique to the sand dunes of the Colorado Desert where harvester ants are an important food source.

Peninsular Bighorn sheep defy gravity leaping about canyon walls. Photo by Loretta Currie

The coyote with his lonely cry is synonymous with the Southwest desert. It's one of the most commonly seen of the large desert mammals. It holds a special place in the American Indian tradition. Native American mythology is filled with coyote stories that were passed down from one generation to the next. In Cahuilla legend, coyote was the first animal. After World Maker created the earth, he made coyote to help him populate the world. In modern times Wile E. Coyote chases, but never catches, the roadrunner.

Coyote

A tawny, eight-foot mountain lion prowls the night looking for prey. He's shy and secretive but afraid of nothing. After all, he's the king; the top of the food chain.

Listen to the desert at night. A thirty pound bobcat intimidates with a fearsome growl as if to substitute volume for size. A raven's raspy caw echoes through canyons. Atop a palm tree, barn owlets in their nest wheeze *shhhtttt sht sht sht shhhtttt* like a Rain Bird sprinkler gone mad.

Mountain Lion

The fact is a desert is a place receiving an annual rainfall of less than ten inches. The average rainfall in the Phoenix area (Sonora Desert) is 7.11 inches. The Coachella Valley (Colorado Desert) averages 3-5 inches per year. Characteristics of a desert are:

- an arid climate,
- extreme temperatures. A range of forty degrees between day and night is not un-common.
- Winds strong enough to shift sand dunes, strip the paint off your car, and give you dermabrasion on the cheap.

Bobcat

The Desert is Fragile

California ground squirrel

The soil is of great importance to human life. We must treat it with respect. A heavy footstep can destroy subterranean life and compact the earth. However, the worst damage is done by off-road vehicles. As they race across the land they have the potential to harm both plants and animals directly, as well as to modify desert ecosystems, making them less habitable. These vehicles scar the land forever. It breaks my heart to see how they crush plants, cover them with soil, or expose their roots. I get teary-eyed when I think about the run-over wildlife, the collapsed burrows, and the damage to seasonal pools. Soil compaction reduces water availability and affects plants' ability to root and germinate and animals' ability to burrow.

Below the soil surface life is active. In the desert, most activity takes place below ground. An extensive root system sprawls to soak up every drop of precious moisture and serves as an anchor against strong desert winds. Plants grow down before growing up. Soil algae and molds, with their interlacing filaments and mycelia, crust the surface of desert soil and help to hold it against wind and rain. Their carbon and nitrogen enhance growing conditions for other plants.

Animals contribute their part to a healthy earth. Burrowing by kangaroo rats provide a remarkable amount of fertilizer. When kangaroo rats leave, other animals move in. Abandoned burrows are taken over by pocket mice, grasshopper mice, ground squirrels, cottontails, as well as snakes and lizards. The droppings of these small animals push the nitrate value still higher.

Kangaroo rat. Photo by www.desertusa.com

The soil serves as a sanctuary. The small burrowing owl takes shelter from daytime heat underground. The desert tortoise buries her eggs in the soil.

Burrowing owl Photo: www.Desertusa.com

Desert plants are outstandingly adapted to their environment. Most desert vegetation has small leaves which reduce evaporation. The thorns of cacti are actually modified leaves. The ribs of some euphorbia and cacti direct any available moisture to the roots. Many desert plants have needle-like spines to discourage predation.

When I work in my garden, I always feel I should be wearing a suit of armor to protect my skin against my beautiful, but often lethal plants. There's nothing soft about the desert. However, the beauty and the rough majesty compensate for scratches and pain. The desert is truly generous when given the slightest encouragement, such as a little spring rain or some supplemental irrigation.

Beavertail cactus (*Opuntia basilaris*)

Water is a Precious Commodity

Murray Canyon, Palm Springs

Water is the sole substance to sustain life. It is a finite resource. When I moved to the desert, everybody I talked to assured me that there was plenty of water; the aquifers were close to the surface. Since then the valley floor in Palm Desert has sunk eighteen inches due to depletion of groundwater. The greatest amount of water is used in landscaping. We can band together and reverse that trend by using native plants in our landscape, in other words, gardening with nature.

The Colorado Desert supports a great diversity of plants. These plants have adapted to the desert's harsh conditions over thousands of years. They are used to temperature extremes, intense sunlight, low humidity, drying winds, and alkaline soils. Many native plants belong to the pea family and naturally add nitrogen to the soil.

Desert plants require little water. They are uniquely adapted to absorb and retain the slightest bit of moisture, whether from the soil or from humidity in the atmosphere. Their extensive root system absorbs available moisture and the small size of their leaves minimizes evaporation. Some have a taproot searching deep for groundwater. The taproot of a mesquite tree, for example, has been measured at 120 feet. Others have roots close to the surface, spreading far and wide searching for water. The creosote bush, to further insure survival, has both a taproot and spreading roots. Each leaf of the creosote bush consists of a set of three small leaves. During prolonged drought it will drop the largest of the small leaves. If the drought continues, it'll drop the next set, and so on, enabling it to go without water for a very long time.

Creosote leaves

It reproduces by cloning as well as by scattering seeds. In Lucerne Valley lives a creosote bush that has been carbon dated and is shown to be more than 12,000 years old. How's that for survival!

Some desert plants fold their leaves and turn them away from the hot sun while others have leaves covered with tiny hairs, much like us wearing a hat during the heat of the day. Brittlebush (*Encelia farinosa*) is an example. Its leaves are actually green but a covering of tiny white hair gives them a silvery appearance. If water is plentiful it sheds the hair and you see green leaves. It's a small, rounded shrub about three feet high and as wide. From March through May, yellow, daisy-like flowers rise on slender stems above the foliage.

Brittlebush (*Encelia farinosa*). Notice how leaves on bottom are green from moisture condensed on the rocks.

I've seen the brown foothills of San Jacinto turn a dazzling yellow with brittlebush flowers after winter rains. Birds and other desert animals feed on the seeds. Native Americans used the resin exuded from the stems as glue. They also chewed it as a treatment for many body aches. Early missionaries burned the resin for incense.

The biggest problem for desert plants is over watering; too much water causes weak and floppy growth. It can spoil a garden; making its plants soft and dependant, lacking stamina and backbone. Disease problems may occur. Remember that a plant wilting from too little water is easier to revive than one rotting from an excess of water. Close planting is a water saver since it shades the ground around the plants. The ideal time to irrigate is early morning. This way the plants have water to carry them through the heat of the day.

Soil, exposure, temperature, humidity, and wind are all factors to consider when deciding how much or how little to water. There are no hard and fast rules. Stroll around your garden, observe your plants, and they'll tell you when they are stressed and need a drink. When your plants are thirsty don't just give them a thimbleful; saturate the soil. They will reward you by sinking their roots deep and eventually require water less often.

I live on an alluvial fan with coarse, sandy soil that drains quickly. I have set my irrigation system to water three times a week for twenty minutes during the warm weather. Occasionally I notice some plants showing signs of wilt so I'll leave a hose near the base to run very slowly for a couple of hours. This allows water to penetrate deep into the soil. In the cooler month I irrigate once every two or three weeks depending on the weather, but always for the same amount of time.

Installing an efficient irrigation system with individual outlets for each plant or a drip system instead of overhead sprinklers entails an initial cost but it's worth it in the long run. When I stopped watering sidewalks and tiled paths my water bill dropped by more than sixty percent. I've dug in some stone saucers in various places to catch any extra water so that butterflies will have a place to puddle and birds can enjoy a drink. A fountain in the garden is a pleasant feature and it doesn't use much water. The chatter of water adds another layer to the sounds in my garden like a distant flute in a piano concert.

An old bathtub gets a new life as a fishpond in the garden

Gardening with nature takes little effort. Treat your garden with benign neglect. Don't be too vigilant about cleanup but leave some dead leaves and brush in a remote corner for wildlife shelter. Add a little irrigation during the hot, dry weather, and your garden will flourish. Nature takes care of itself.

A graveled surface with some desert plantings can be very effective.

Does a Lawn Belong in the Desert?

Personally I prefer a symphony of birdsong underscored with the buzzing of bees and the gentle whistle of wind brushing through leaves instead of a discordant trumpeting of lawnmowers and the drone of blowers.

Once upon a time a lawn was a status symbol. So were fur coats. Think of all the effort going into keeping up a lawn. First you water (a lot) to make it grow; then you crew cut and the clippings end up in our landfills. You fertilize to make it lush but that also feeds the weeds. So you spray it with herbicides and pesticides effectively sterilizing the soil, killing all the bugs nourishing the earth before the poisons seep into the groundwater.

But hold on. This is not all. In the desert you need two lawns—a summer lawn (mostly Bermuda grass) and a winter lawn (rye grass). In early fall the summer lawn is scalped and reseeded and watered two to five times a day. This is a difficult time for asthma sufferers and causes respiratory problems for many. And there is more. One of the great attributes of the desert is the clean air. Running a lawnmower for one hour causes as much air pollution as driving a gas-guzzling SUV for 350 miles. Blowers I find offensive. A broom and a rake are not high-tech tools but they do the job. They are as efficient as a blower and a lot less smelly and noisy. Allergy sufferers take note: low-tech tools don't spread pollen the way a blower does.

An expanse of a rolling green, weed free lawn is beautiful. So is a leopard coat. Let the leopard keep his spots and leave the turf to wetter, more temperate climes. A lawn is safe and conventional (sterile and boring!). Release the artist within you: be bold and daring; consider lawn alternatives.

A bold use of pebbles and boulders can be dramatic. Organic or inorganic mulches can substitute for lawn. Mulches help to conserve water, keep the ground surface cool, and protect the soil. They also cut down on weeds thereby saving you time and energy.

If your taste veers east, say the sparse restraint of a Japanese landscape, then consider planting a clump of deer grass. This perennial grass is native to the Colorado Desert. It is a warm season perennial that forms dense clumps from the base. From July to October it produces one foot long flowering spikes above a three foot high mound of foliage. The one-and one-half-foot long and one-eighth-inch wide leaves are rough textured and stay green all year. Deer grass has striking foundation form. A clump of Deer grass benefits wildlife. A mass planting creates a striking effect. It is drought tolerant and a fast grower.

Deer grass (*Muhlenbergia rigens*)

Many plants make excellent groundcovers. White Bur-sage (*Ambrosia dumosa*) is an evergreen shrub about two feet high and three feet wide. It can be massed or placed in a random manner. As it ages it develops a delicate open appearance. Paperbag bush, also known as Bladder-sage (*Salazaria mexicana*), might be another choice. Paperbag bush (the name refers to the fruit, an inflated light tan pouch) can reach three feet in height with a similar spread. It blooms in spring with purple and white half-inch flowers.

Verbena

Verbena has trumpet-shaped, fragrant flowers that bloom from February through May. They are hairy creepers with flower stalks up to ten inches long and stems trail up to three feet. After abundant rain Sand verbena carpets desert washes.

Take advantage of all options for your own garden.

Hawk taking a rest at the poolside

A Garden Is More Than Plants

A garden is a sustainable environment that aims to please all senses and enriches the spirit. The gardener is a self-appointed guardian of the land; a preserver of the unique character of the desert. The extraordinary landscape of the Colorado Desert with its rugged mountains, gentle plains, and sandy washes supports more than 800 species of flowering plants as well as numerous birds and animals. As more of the desert is devoured by development, it is crucial that individual residents protect the spirit and characteristics of the desert. The way to do this is by cultivating native vegetation which helps sustain the wildlife that is losing its natural environment. Otherwise, our beloved desert will indeed become a wasteland as barren as an asphalt parking lot.

Verbena, Penstemon, milkweed

By choosing from the enormous array of native plants available you can fulfill both aesthetic and functional needs requiring very little maintenance. Whether you desire a lush and luxurious garden or a landscape that is stark and dramatic, you can find the appropriate plants to make the garden uniquely yours while still retaining a sense of place.

You can make your garden a wildlife habitat. Life in the desert is tough. Struggle for survival is fierce and any action you take is welcome. As the natural environment shrinks we can make amends by providing food, water, and shelter in the way we plan our garden. Such actions present us with payback. Our outdoor environment comes alive. The increased range of birds, insects, and small mammals act as a natural biological control. They devour garden pests without the use of chemicals.

When I moved to the desert I had a monthly pest control service to keep my house bug and insect free. I had been told that was the thing to do. But between services the flying and crawling pests still invaded my house. I don't use screens and keep most of my windows and doors open so I was partly to blame for the invasion. However, when I converted to gardening with nature I cancelled the pest control service and bought a fly swatter. To my surprise, I discovered fewer intruders in my house than when I had the exterminator come. My wildlife did the job much more efficiently. I haven't had to use the fly swatter even once. Each insect and each disease has its own natural enemy.

Each of us can encourage a broader diversity of wildlife to ensure a healthy and ecological balance. An added advantage is the pleasure we derive from observing the life affirming activities in our garden. Gardening is good for the soul; gardening is good for the body. It puts the mind at ease and relieves stress while also protecting the environment.

"Why has not man a microscopic eye? For this plain reason: man is not a fly." —Alexander Pope 1688-1744

Little Boys Like Bugs

Baby squirrel

Kids live close to the ground. They notice things that are too far away from an adult's perspective. Little boys in particular seem mesmerized by creepy-crawlies. They pick all sorts of living things out of the dirt to touch and examine the wonder of them all in detail.

Many insects and bugs are beneficial. They nourish soil and pollinate plants. When I see aphids in my garden, I don't panic. I wait for the ladybugs to follow. Aphids are seasonal and short-lived. Ladybugs love to eat them.

My gardening is up close and personal. Nose close to the earth, I notice emerging weeds and pull them before they get a strong foothold. I immediately see if plants are suffering from stress due to too much water or too little water and take corrective action. What's more, I get a close look at the multitude of fascinating bugs and insects that thrive in and on the soil.

Praying mantis

I remember the praying mantis from years on the East coast where there was a hefty fine for killing one. Surprised to see a praying mantis among my plants here, I stopped to admire this three inch long predator praying over my plants while ridding them of insects feeding on the leaves. Indiscriminate eaters, they devour beneficial and harmful insects alike. Not to worry, though, they too have enemies, such as birds, to keep their population in control.

The praying mantis is closely related to the roach. It is a carnivorous insect that waits motionless for the right sized insect to come within reach. At rest it holds its forelegs together and assumes a humble posture as if praying. The mantis eats its prey while it is still alive and always goes straight for the insect's neck to quickly stop its struggling. Besides insects the mantis also eats other invertebrates such as beetles, butterflies, spiders, crickets, and grasshoppers. They breed in the summer and, after mating, the female will lay groups of twelve to four hundred eggs in a frothy liquid that turns into a hard protective shell. Small mantises emerge in the spring and their first meal is often a sibling. It takes an entire summer for them to mature to adulthood. After mating the female commonly devours the male. Praying mantises occur naturally over a broad range of climate and geography. In some cultures the mantis is considered holy. It is believed that if you are lost and see a mantis, it will lead you home if you go in the direction the mantis is facing.

Milkweed bugs mating
Photo by Scott Camazine-Penn State University Dept. of Entomology

I've been able to identify a milkweed bug. It feeds on seeds and tissues of the milkweed plant. It has a positive impact on the ecosystem in that it is one of a small group of insects that have the ability to tolerate the toxic compounds in the milkweed plant and therefore are important in regulating populations of this plant. Of course, if you are cultivating milkweed to attract butterflies you might consider this a negative impact.

I've experienced some unfortunate encounters with ants while picnicking. They always seem to appear in large numbers. Ants are nature's cleaning crew and are useful for clearing out insect pests and aerating the soil.

A lot of other insects and bugs are still a mystery to me. Since I don't know if they are "good" or "bad," I leave them alone. Lizards, bats, and birds are indiscriminate eaters and will make sure to keep an ecological balance.

One day I thought I saw a dragon. Well, a small one (for a dragon). I came across this fat, bright green creature with red spots and a horn on the tail end. It was about five inches long. It was gorging on my evening primroses. I must have alarmed it as much as it alarmed me because it reared up its head in a threatening sphinx-like posture and emitted a thick, green substance from its mouth.

Hornworm

I called on a knowledgeable friend who identified the "dragon" as a hornworm, the voracious larvae of a white-lined sphinx moth. I learned that another name for this moth is hummingbird moth or the hawk moth. Its hovering, swift flight pattern and its size (wingspans ranging from two to eight inches) sometimes makes people mistake it for a hummingbird. Among the largest flying insects of the desert they are busy pollinators of evening primroses and other fragrant night blooming flowers, thereby guaranteeing future flowers.

Evening primrose

Every day is a day of discovery. I reflect on my early days in the desert more than twenty years ago when, in the summertime, Palm Springs resembled a ghost town. In those days everything was unfamiliar and, at times, frightening—like the time a tarantula strolled into my bedroom. I panicked. I jumped on top of my bed from where I could reach my phone and dial 911.

While waiting for rescue I ran outside and closed the doors behind me. By the time the police arrived the tarantula was gone—no arrest. I'm sure I provided some entertainment on a dull evening.

The big, hairy, scary looking tarantula is actually a shy creature and harmless to humans. Tarantulas live in burrows which they line with a silk webbing to prevent sand from trickling in. They only reach sexual maturity at three to nine years of age. The male dies shortly after mating, possibly eaten by the female, while the female has a lifespan of twenty-five to forty years. It's a solitary being. It does not build a web like other spiders but hunts its prey of insects and small lizards. Its main enemy is the tarantula wasp. Now, the rare times I encounter a tarantula, I wonder if it is an old lady of thirty-something or a teenager with raging hormones.

I used to be terrified of snakes. One day I looked out my window and saw a snake slithering across the ground. I called on animal control. When they came, the snake was long gone. By my description, about three feet long with black and white bands, it was identified as a king snake—not only harmless but actually beneficial to have around as it'll keep rattlesnakes away. To overcome my fear I would visit the snake exhibit at the Palm Springs Desert Museum (now Palm Springs Art Museum) where I stood for hours watching the reptiles and learning about them.

Most snakes here in the desert are harmless and even venomous snakes will not attack unless provoked or stepped on and even then they'll conserve their venom for more edible prey. The way to tell a venomous snake from a non-venomous one is by its head: a venomous snake, such as the Western diamondback rattlesnake and the sidewinder, has a triangular head to accommodate the poisonous fangs.

I've come a long way since then. The unknown has become known and with knowledge has come awareness and understanding. The unfamiliar has become familiar; it no longer frightens but fills me with wonder.

Why Gardening with Nature?

Landscapes are living systems that change over time. Watching the landscape grow and change is a satisfying reward to gardening. Compelling reasons for gardening with nature are that it is life sustaining and ecologically sound.

• Saving energy

Working in conjuncture with nature instead of trying to conquer it or mold it means less labor. Weeds need water to grow. If you only water the plants you want, weeds will not have a chance to sprout and you don't have to weed as much.

When buying plants I prefer the one gallon size. I don't have to dig a big hole (saving my energy). Several years ago I bought a one gallon Texas Ranger (Leucophyllum frutescens "Green Cloud"). With its purple-violet flowers I thought it would look marvelous in the front of my border. I turned my back and when I looked again it was eight feet tall with an eight-foot spread. I still love it even though it overpowered my smaller plants that eventually succumbed. I love the fact that it'll produce an abundance of flowers in the slightest bit of humidity but I learned my lesson. The speed with which the smaller plants grow will amaze you.

By the way, Texas Ranger is not native to the Colorado Desert but to Texas as the name implies. However, I've included it because it has proven itself as a survivor here and it is beneficial to our local wildlife. Bees feed on the flowers and quail seek sanctuary beneath its branches. It doesn't spread so is no threat to native plants. It is a good choice for a hedge or a privacy screen.

Buying the smaller size is cheaper and there's less chance of transplanting shock than with a larger size plant. Beware, though, that small plants don't stay small. Always consider its mature size. Is this variety going to overwhelm the space?

Texas Ranger that started from a one-gallon pot

Friends almost stopped coming to my house when the pair of agaves flanking my entrance outgrew their space and attacked them with their needle sharp points (it kept solicitors away as well). I had to call in professional help to have them removed. It was expensive. I saved some agave pups to plant in large pots where they stay contained.

Agave in pot

If you love a plant consider whether you have the space for it or if you must constantly prune it to keep it small. Save yourself some work: buy plants to suit the space. If you have placed plants where they can grow to their full size and retain their natural shape and grouped your plants according to their needs, your landscape should require little attention. The main long-term tasks will be weeding and the occasional pruning away dead branches. Most of the natural gardener's time will be spent watching the show.

• Saving money

Every year billions of dollars are devoted to halt change in the landscape. Trees are topped and shrubs are sheared. Chemicals are applied to force plants to behave a certain way. The ground is raked and blown to keep leaves and other organic matter from accumulating.

An attractive conventional landscape is expensive to build and it remains expensive throughout its existence. The initial cost of installing a natural garden might be similar but it starts its payback in the second or third year when watering is reduced, maintenance becomes minimal, and much of the insect activity becomes self-regulating.

Native plants are adapted to the local soil and don't need fertilizer. You can spend your money on plant material instead of chemicals. Consider letting your palm trees retain their skirts as an alternative to hiring labor to cut the dead fronds. This way you'll provide shelter and nesting material for birds of many kinds. Birds will eat the seeds and insects and you won't need any other pest control. Bats, too, might be attracted; they are voracious insect eaters. When seeds drop, ground squirrels are happy to do the clean up.

Deciduous trees planted on the south and west side of the house will provide shade in the summer and invite the warmth of sunrays in the cool months, which means less artificial heating and cooling.

• Saving the environment
Our role as gardeners is to aid the natural processes that rejuvenate the soil and support the plants that grow in it. Over time, as the landscape matures, we should expect it to require fewer resources and less activity on our part.

Integrating the garden into the landscape so it is truly in harmony with its setting adds a sense of place which is important for a successful landscape design.

Mourning dove

By planting native plants you'll attract and sustain the native wildlife that is losing its habitat due to human advance. You can restore a small part of the desert ecosystem by providing shelter, nesting material, and food.

Besides saving energy and money you'll aide in preserving our desert for future generations, so that they, too, can feast their eyes on nature's dramatic productions featuring our furry, feathered, and scaly friends.

Baby squirrels are exploring their world

Designing the Landscape

It is possible to create a spectacular garden using only native plants. But you don't have to be a purist to create an ecological, beneficial environment. Many of us already have an established garden. Over time you can convert a traditional landscape to a natural desert garden which will grant enjoyment on many levels. When plants die or outgrow their space, you can replace them with plants native to the Colorado Desert.

For a strong vertical accent, a planting of Desert milkweed is an excellent choice.

Desert milkweed (*Asclepias subulate*) is close to being lost in the wild due to development. It's an essential food plant for the larvae of the Monarch butterfly and the Queen butterfly.

Painted lady butterfly

Butterflies are plant specific about where to lay their eggs. The plant has to be able to nourish the emerging larvae. Without milkweeds we will lose the Monarchs and the Queen butterflies. The Painted lady butterfly larvae feed on Desert Mallow and various thistles but once it metamorphoses to a butterfly it, too, feeds on Milkweed.

Desert Milkweed is sun loving and drought resistant once it has been established. Its slender, gray-green stems grow vertically to four feet with a two foot spread. From spring through fall, flat-topped clusters of pale yellow flowers top each stem. When ripe, the three inch ornamental horn-shaped pods split open to disperse a silvery fluff of seeds.

Milkweed seed pod
Photo by Gay Wehrli

A well designed garden is a treat for all senses. I meander through my garden and feast my eyes on color and form. I touch a rock warmed by the sun. I feel the soft, furry leaves of a brittlebush and brush against the rough trunk of a palm tree. I breathe the pungent scent of a Creosote bush after a brief rain. I inhale the ambrosia of Datura flowers at night, the perfume of Smoketree blossoms in early summer, and the wonderful aroma of various sages. I munch on the sweet seeds dropping from palm trees and taste the bitter leaves of the Creosote.

In the mornings, I take my coffee outside and listen to the rustle of leaves and grasses and the wind whispering through the landscape with wildlife adding its own chorus. Birds are natural conversationalists; I eavesdrop on their prattle and feel a profound connection.

Style of Landscape

Hummingbird at left, Cooper's hawk in front.

If I were presented with a plot of bare dirt, I'd sit down with a large sheet of graph paper and a pencil, surround myself with gardening books, and meticulously plan my garden—a tree here, a berm there, some shrubs and flowers. I would reference my books, make a list of the plants I required, and send somebody else to do the shopping. When I enter a nursery temptation itches, begging to be scratched. As pleasing as the plants may be, impulse buying from the nursery doesn't add up to a palpable whole. In theory my garden would be perfect. However, gardening is a work in progress. A garden is forever changing; nothing stays the same.

I didn't start with a blank slate when I bought my house. It already had a garden. I decided to approach my landscape like a painter tackling a canvas. However, even a painter does some planning or utter chaos will result.

Ask yourself what kind of landscape you want. Don't let limitations of space intimidate you. Whether you live in a palace or a mobile home, as long as you have a patch of dirt, you can create a garden. Any area that is open to the sky can become a garden.

A trio consisting of an ocotillo, an agave, and a low-growing cactus will fill a small space with great impact. For a softer look and continuous bloom you can add some desert marigolds.

Ocotillo, Opuntia, Palo Verde with Desert Spoon in foreground

In a large garden think tree—a Palo verde tree or a mesquite for filtered shade, a desert willow for orchid-like flowers in the summer. You can simulate a desert wash with sand and stones and a scattering of wildflowers. The possibilities are endless. Using native plants doesn't limit your options. The Colorado Desert hosts more than eight hundred species of flowering plants.

Indian blanket flower (*Gaillardia*)

Indoor/outdoor living is a major bonus to life in the desert. A relationship between garden and house is vital. In other words, consider the architecture of your home when designing your outdoor space. Your home should blend into nature without trying to dominate the sweeping and dramatic landscape. You can link environment, landscape, and house into an interconnected whole. I like to think of it as a marriage between the inside and the outdoors—a close relationship between house and garden in both style and atmosphere. Proportion is important. A smaller garden should be simple in design.

Cottonwood tree

Towering sycamore trees and cottonwoods can overwhelm the typical one-story south-western style home. A lot of small plants on a large property with a massive house will look out of place.

To achieve a sense of unity you can carry your indoor décor on to the landscape. Consider extending your indoor flooring, seamlessly connecting the interior of the house to the outdoors. The flooring in my house is Saltillo tiles; when I extended it to my outside patios I had an immediate relationship. I continued the link by using equipale chairs on a covered patio, the same kind of chairs that I have in my dining room.

Covered patio extends living space

A colorful painting and some metal lizards on the wall completed the furnishings. Then I added some large pots filled with flowers to bring the garden even closer. With the French doors open, it's as if my home has doubled in size. When I am inside looking out there's a smooth transition. I've brought the outdoors in and the indoors out, a continuous connection with nature.

Palo Verde tree

Survey your garden from your house through doors and windows. Does the view please you? Maybe some rearranging is in order. Now stroll into the garden and take a good look. Do the architecture and the landscape form a harmonic whole? A formal garden might best echo a traditional house. A modern house might best be complemented by a stark, spiky landscape.

No matter what style you prefer, you'll find native plant material to suit your taste. So go ahead, establish a sense of place and express yourself.

When considering a color scheme choose colors to complement the exterior as well as the interior of the house. When viewed from the distance, a grouping of colors, or tones of a color, is most effective. In the desert the vivid landscape and the purity of light seem to beg for strong colors to stand out against brilliant blue skies, fleecy white clouds, umber mountains, the amber valley floor, and the turquoise and peach sunsets. Many desert plants have yellow flowers, luminous against a blue sky. Personally, I love the look of the lacy foliage of a Palo verde tree. Its small, brilliant yellow flowers contrast the coarse texture of an Ocotillo plant with its bright orange fluorescence and dark green leaves. For more texture and color a low-growing cactus would anchor the planting.

Ocotillo bloom

While yellow is the predominant flower color, it is not the only one. You'll find desert flowers in the whole spectrum of the color wheel: yellow-orange-bronze petals of Indian blanket flowers; some sages have scarlet flowers, others have flowers cobalt blue or the palest blue; the flowers of the Indigo bush are the deepest purple.

Sage (*Salvia greggii*)

Penstemon

Sage flower (*Salvia farinacea*)

Nothing blooms all the time (except, of course, Desert Marigold); every flower has its season. In nature there are other sources of color.

California poppy

Tecoma stans and desert marigold

The foliage of desert vegetation varies from pale gray through blue gray to a multitude of greens, from the yellow-green leaves of a Mesquite tree to the rich, dark green of the creosote bush. Fruit and seeds present color and interest. Palo Verde trees have twisted green branches and gnarled, light green trunks that turn a mottled grayish brown with age. The sculptural trunk of the Mesquite tree is the deep, rich color of dark chocolate. Some trees have white bark.

Color alone does not a garden make. Form and texture add structure to your design. Here again, the diverse desert vegetation presents you with a wide range of choices. Consider vertical or horizontal lines, round or a spiky form, soft or sharp shapes—the choices are endless. Balancing color with texture and sculptural plant forms makes a garden reflect the seasons. Bring out the artist within you and have fun experimenting.

On the Wild Side

Prickly pear

Plant wild but don't go wild or you'll end up with a vegetative clutter. A wild garden needs careful maintenance. If you choose plants appropriate for the space and place them in a location of their preference—sun or shade—upkeep becomes minimal. You'll want to remove dead branches and withered foliage for an orderly look. In addition, an occasional shaping of trees and shrubs to achieve the required natural form might be necessary. Newly planted vegetation requires regular water until roots are well established—normally the first year after planting.

You might want to remove spent flowers (deadheading) to keep the plants blooming for a longer period. I let my desert marigolds reseed and I am always pleasantly surprised when these perky flowers pop up in unexpected places. However, I'm vigilant about removing anything unwanted—what I consider weeds. Occasionally I have volunteers; those are plants sprouting from seeds brought into my garden by birds, animals, or the wind. If they fit into the overall landscape and are native, they are volunteers and get to stay; if they are exotics, they don't belong in my garden. I consider them weeds and I pull them before they have a chance to spread. I want to prevent my landscape from degenerating into an untidy collection of plant material.

Simplicity is the keynote in design, the treble. Diversity is the bass. You'll want variety in order to create interest. Unity and variety are complimentary parts of a whole. Strong lines and repetition are unifying elements; a mix of balancing plants provides interest. To attract many kinds of wildlife you'll want an assortment of plants. Brightly colored, tubular flowers attract hummingbirds; bees love all kinds of sages. Butterflies feed on flat daisy-like flowers.

Simple lines with a focal point of interest are preferable. In nature, plants grow widely spaced in order to limit competition for available resources. You can duplicate that look in the garden but remember that a garden is ever-changing. Plants grow and stretch with time. Plants die. In a garden setting with some irrigation there's less competition; plants will grow faster than in a natural setting.

In riparian areas you'll see a denser growth with various species massing together. Mass plantings keep the ground cool. In a garden setting it also helps cut down on weeds. You can create an oasis by planting a trio of palm trees around a water feature such as a small pond or a fountain with some low-growing Penstemon or a grouping of Desert Fuchsia (*Zauscheneria california ssp. latifolia*) with its bright red tubular flowers that are sure to attract hummingbirds. Plant a tree like Mesquite, Palo Verde, or Desert Willow then add Arrow-weed with its showy lavender flowers. These plants grow naturally in sandy washes where there is moisture. An area close to the house is the logical spot for an oasis. The extra water helps cool the living spaces.

If you don't like the empty look of a garden newly planted with immature plants, think about filling in the vacant spaces with movable objects. Fill in with rocks and garden art. I use the rocks I dig out of the soil to fashion a freeform "river" rippling among the plants, like a dry creek.

A river of rocks

Clockwise from left to right: Golden barrel cactus, Mexican bird of paradise, Opuntia, Yucca, Verbena

Large rocks make their own statement.
Boulders help keep soil from eroding while creating moisture condensing niches. They strike a dramatic note in the desert landscape.

A house with little architectural distinction attains drama by bold use of large rocks

"A garden without a statue is like a sentence without a verb."

Nature Abhors a Vacuum

Waiting for chosen plants to reach maturity tests a gardener's patience. It's tempting to add more plants to vacant space for a comprehensive look. However, considering how fast plants grow in the desert, it's a short-lived pleasure that only creates work for the gardener and green waste to our landfills. Instead, consider an over-sized pot strategically placed—or maybe a grouping of pots in different sizes—and you've achieved instant gratification.

Many artists create outstanding works of art suitable for a garden setting. You can pick pieces made of metal, stone, or glass; you can select natural tones, rusted iron or cast bronze, or sculpture in brilliant colors. The choices are endless.

Metal sculpture by Daniela Came

At left, painted metal lady by Daniela Came, in foreground, bronze "the egg" by Finnish artist.

Stainless steel "Penelope" with colored glass by Michael Paul Thiry

Rusted metal Shaman

"The difference between a flower and a weed is judgment."

A Thorn in the Flesh

Nut-grass (*Cyperus rotundus*)

Nut-grass is my pet peeve. It is indigenous to Africa and Europe and is known as a weed in more than ninety countries. I've learned that it's a worldwide problem in all climates.

Nut-grass is bright green sedge with three very upright pointy leaves sprouting from a central base. As the plant develops it starts sending out "nuts" underground. These nuts store nutrients and keep sprouting until they run out of food. They soak up all moisture and change the texture of the soil, leaving it as dry and lifeless as dead wood ashes. They are a tough competitor for ground resources and the roots release a substance that is harmful to other plants. It grows extremely fast—think "Jack and the Beanstalk" and you get the picture.

At first I tried digging it out but that only seemed to make it grow faster in the loose, disturbed soil. Much against my beliefs I resorted to herbicides. Round-Up acted like a fertilizer. Then somebody told me about Manage, an herbicide only available to professionals, so I had to enlist the help of a gardener. He applied it several times at weekly intervals. It helped some, but it didn't eradicate this invasive, perennial weed. Now I'm using a low-tech approach: pulling it up as soon as it appears and hoping I'll eventually weaken it. However, that means looking every day and knowing I won't be finished until the last shoot is gone. Until then, I continue my daily nut-grass patrol.

If you happen to discover this pest in your garden, I recommend going after it immediately. Don't let it get a foothold if you can avoid it.

In nature every cloud has a silver lining. Despite its nasty reputation, nut-grass does have some positive aspects. In China it was used in traditional medicine as a regulating herb. The plant is mentioned in the ancient Indian medicine Charaka Samhita ca. A.D. 100. Arabs in the land of Israel traditionally used roasted tubers while they were still hot, or hot ashes from burnt tubers, to treat wounds, bruises, and carbuncles.

Modern alternative medicine practitioners recommend using the plant to treat nausea, fever, and inflammation. It's used for pain control, muscle relaxation and many other disorders.

The tubers are edible and have nutritional value although with a bitter taste. In Africa they are used as food in times of famine.

Despite its redeeming features I don't want it taking over my garden. It does not belong in the Colorado Desert.

In the Pink

Queen's wreath (*Antigonon leptopus*)

A garden filled with healthy plants is a beautiful garden. It is also a garden requiring little maintenance as healthy plants are less prone to disease and insect damage.

Health starts with the soil. The desert soil is alkaline so it makes sense to choose plants that thrive in this kind of soil. During my early years in the desert I tried growing camellia and azalea, both acid-loving plants; even with much pampering they didn't survive. I agonized over their slow demise.

Native plants have adapted to the desert soil. Many belong to the pea family (legumes) and produce their own nitrogen so fertilizer becomes unnecessary. Insects, bugs, and small mammals aerate the soil, providing a fertile base for the plants to establish a vigorous root system.

New landscape with gravel mulch

To mulch or not to mulch—that's the question. To me the answer is a resounding yes. It keeps the soil healthy. Mulch limits soil compaction; it keeps soil cool in the heat of summer and insulates plant roots from heat and cold, enhancing growth and vigor. It prevents moisture from evaporating. Mulch applied four to six inches deep suppresses weeds. Finally, it makes the landscape look more finished, unifying spaces until plants fill in and create continuity.

There are basically two kinds of mulch: organic and inorganic. Organic mulches eventually break down, releasing nutrients and creating better soil. It will need to be replaced periodically. Woodchips and bark chips are organic. In my garden I use "Nature Scapes," a color enhanced mulch by Scotts. This terracotta colored, fade resistant mulch is made from natural forest products that are by-products of the timber industry. The drawback is that it tends to track into the house.

Inorganic mulches such as stones, gravel, and decomposed granite last a long time. A combination of gravel and larger stones creates interest. Decomposed granite is commonly used for a neat, orderly look. A disadvantage to inorganic mulch is that is absorbs and reflects heat.

Desert Trees

Mesquite

I no longer give my adult children birthday presents. Instead I plant a tree in their honor. For each of my grandchildren's first day of school I planted a tree seedling in my garden. To my delight the kids have developed a keen interest in hearing at regular intervals how much their "baby trees" have grown.

Trees inhale carbon dioxide and exhale oxygen. They are the backbone in the landscape. Trees create micro climates. Broad spreading canopies trap heat and act as a natural shade cloth sheltering plants below and providing both winter and summer protection. Allow their canopy to spread; don't thin their branches excessively. Over-pruning exposes a tree's woody material by removing layers of insulating foliage and smaller plants beneath the canopy are vulnerable to frost and sun. In nature, plants gain protection in groupings.

Besides providing a place for birds to roost and nest, trees also offer shade and wind protection. Deciduous trees planted on the west or south sides of your house shade it during the hot months while allowing the sun to penetrate during the colder time of the year, acting as a thermal blanket. Trees can be used as a sculptural accent.

The trees included in this chapter are ones most commonly seen in the desert and my personal favorites. They are not the only native trees.

Shortly after I had moved to the desert I visited the Thousand Palms Oasis (now the Coachella Valley Preserve). It was like entering a church. There was the kind hush you experience upon crossing the threshold to a cathedral. Rippling brooks meandered among majestic palms, providing a welcome shade on that hot August day. Desert pupfish filled the shallow waterways and birds trilled overhead.

California fan palm (*Washingtonia filifera*) is the only palm native to California. Out of 2500 palm species it is also the only one where the leaves will adhere to the trunk during its lifetime. It produces a date-like edible fruit which is treasured by birds and small mammals alike.

The California fan palm plays an important supporting role in nature. In spring the beautiful orange and black hooded orioles strip fibers off the leaves to sew a nest onto the underside of a leaf. Great horned owls and barn owls build nests in the skirt formed by the dead leaves. Lizards and bats find shelter in the California fan palm.

The California fan palm was an important resource for the Cahuilla Indians who called it "maul." They would grind the fruit into flour or they made it into a mush. Soaking the fruits produced a sweet drink or they made jelly from the fruit. The spongy pith in the center of the palm was sometimes boiled and eaten; they called it "maul pasun" or "heart of palm."

Native Americans let nothing go to waste. They used leaves of the fan palm in construction for roof thatch. They stripped the leaves and used the fibers for weaving baskets or they braided the fibers into ropes. Leaf fibers were also used to make skirts and sandals.

After the fruit pulp dried, the hard seeds became the preferred fill for gourd rattles.

The California fan palm oases, usually located along earthquake faults, were indicative of important springs. The presence of water made these oases important gathering and habitation sites.

The California fan palm has a lifespan of several hundred years. It grows about one to one-and-a-half feet a year, reaching a height of more than fifty-five feet.

"Wait a minute," cried my friend as she tried to free her clothing snagged on the claw-like thorns of a catclaw acacia during our walk in the desert.

Catclaw acacia (*Acacia greggii*) is the only acacia native to the Colorado Desert. Its thorns, hidden among the gray-green foliage, resemble a cat's claws. For obvious reasons it's also known as "wait-a-minute bush." It is a ten to fifteen feet tall scraggly shrub that spreads to twenty-five feet but by removing the lower foliage you can expose its picturesque and gnarly trunk, pruning it into a small tree. It makes an excellent security plant as well as an attractive accent plant—but make sure you place it well away from walkways.

In spring, fuzzy, pale yellow, two inch long flower spikes perfume the air around Catclaw acacia. The flowers are followed by three-inch long, rust-colored pods. It is deciduous in winter and may also drop its leaves during prolonged drought.

Many small birds and mammals find shelter among these natural armed fortresses and build their nest there. Quail eat the seeds and the flowers are an important source of nectar for bees.

Catclaw acacia

Pods and seeds are bitter. Native Americans boiled pods or soaked beans overnight to make them edible and then ground them into flour. They also used the wood in construction of their dwellings and for firewood.

Catclaw acacia in flower (*Acacia greggii*)

Palo verde (Cercidium species)

Two different species of palo verde trees are native to the Colorado Desert: blue palo verde and littleleaf palo verde. Their delicate leaves are like green lace against a blue sky. The common characteristics of both are green trunk and branches (palo verde means 'green stick'). During drought conditions the tree sheds its leaves to limit water loss but chlorophyll in bark permits photosynthesis to continue.

Both trees have a taproot that goes down as much as two hundredc feet, thus tolerating undergrowth of other plants without interference with its root system.

Bees visit the flowers to yield good honey. Native Americans ground seeds of both trees into flour that they baked into cakes or ate as mush.

I like both trees and would make size the main consideration when choosing between them.

Blue Palo Verde (*Cercidium floridum*) grows fast to a height of thirty feet with as wide a spread. In spring it is covered with clusters of bright yellow flowers that almost hide the intricate pattern of bluish green, spiny branches. A moderately dense shade cools a patio but allows enough light to grow shade tolerant plants beneath.

Birds love the tree for nesting as well as for nourishment, feeding on the flowers and seeds. Desert tortoises have been seen eating the fallen flowers.

Littleleaf Palo Verde (*Cercidium microphyllum*) normally reaches a mature height of twelve feet with a fifteen feet wide canopy. It is similar to blue palo verde but bark and leaves are yellowish green and flowers are a paler yellow. The delicate, almost hazy, look of the foliage contrasts an often very gnarled trunk. Its small size makes it a wonderful specimen tree but keep it away from walkways as the branches end in spines. The flowers and seedpods create some litter so you will not want it near a pool. However, since birds like to nest in this tree and a variety of desert animals feed on the flowers and seeds, I'd want it in a place where I can observe the wildlife activity.

Hummingbird taking a rest in Palo verde tree

Cottonwood (*Populus fremontii*) is a fast growing deciduous tree. This handsome, broad-leaved tree with an open crown is suitable for large spaces. Cottonwood will reach a height of ninety feet at maturity so it's not for small gardens. It has an invasive root system and should be planted at least fifteen feet from house or wall foundations. Also make sure to keep it away from water lines, sewer lines, or septic tanks or their leach lines. Weekly watering is needed unless its roots have tapped into an underground source.

Thick, glossy yellow-green leaves turn bright yellow in fall and remain on the tree practically all winter in the Colorado Desert. Small greenish yellow flowers in long slender catkins appear in spring, followed by masses of cottony seeds that blow about like a down mattress split open.

If you are set on having a cottonwood tree take heart: you can control the height somewhat by letting the tree develop multiple trunks. There are male and female cottonwood trees; male trees have no seeds so they won't be a nuisance.

Cottonwood is an important tree for birds and butterflies so if you have the space by all means plant one. For Halloween I can imagine doing what the Mojave Indians did—use the bark to make skirts.

Desert Willow (*Chilopsis linearis*) belongs to the Bignonia family and is the only member native to California. Its relatives are mostly tropical trees, shrubs, and vines with showy flowers. It is a sprawling shrub or small tree from six to twenty feet tall. Desert Willow is not a true willow but its long, slender leaves make it look like one.

Desert Willows are tap-rooted, flowering trees that can be used close to walls and foundations to shade windows and bring hummingbirds close for viewing. Its medium green fine-textured foliage drops during the winter but from April through September, pink to purple flowers decorate the branches of Desert Willow. The fragrant, ruffled, trumpet-shaped blooms resemble orchids.

This fast-growing tree likes full sun but will grow in partial shade. Once it is established it can survive on the occasional rainfall but for more attractive foliage and flowers it is a good idea to give it supplemental irrigation a couple of times a month during the summer. Desert Willow grants shelter to nesting birds while its seeds supply their food. The nectar is ambrosia for hummingbirds.

Native Americans brewed a pleasant-tasting tea from the dried flowers and seedpods.

However, the wood was the most important part of the plant. The branches are pliable, strong, and highly resistant to decay which made them an important source for construction material in the building of Indian houses. Because of their flexibility they could be used in rectangular as well as domed structures as supporting posts and beams. Another use was in the creation of granaries—large woven baskets—used to hold mesquite pods and other foods collected in large quantities.

Desert willow (Chilopsis linearis)

Ironwood (*Olneya tesota*) has a hard heavy wood that is valued for carving and firewood. This evergreen tree with a spreading crown grows to fifteen to thirty-five feet. Its bark is light gray when young but turning darker as it matures. The foliage is gray-green. In May and June loose clusters of pink-lavender flowers develop into two-inch-long brown pods containing edible seeds that taste somewhat like peanuts.

The natural character of Ironwood is attractive and pruning should be limited to removing dead branches. Its straight half-inch spines make an excellent security screen. Low hanging branches make it suitable for a privacy screen. It often becomes the center of attention in a garden even as it complements other desert plants. It is appropriate in a naturalistic desert setting planted along a wash or shading a patio. It produces little litter so it can be used in a poolside planting.

Native Americans used the wood to make arrowheads. They also ate the seeds after parching them, or they pulverized them to flour from which they made a gruel or cake.

Bighorn sheep and mule deer browse the plant.

Elephant tree (*Bursera microphylla*) was first sighted in the Colorado Desert in 1911. Its exact location became a mystery which led to an organized elephant tree hunt. Seventy-five specimens were located in the Fish Creek area of the Anza-Borrego State Park. Since then other stands have been found in the Santa Rosa Mountains. The trees are usually found in rocky areas and on slopes.

This small tree's swollen trunk with peeling parchment-like bark inspired the common name. Under optimal conditions it can reach a height of twenty to thirty feet with a twenty foot spread. The typical size is six feet by eight feet. It has reddish-brown twigs and dark green foliage. In July and August it blooms with inconspicuous small creamy white flowers. Purplish-blue huckleberry-like fruits hang in a drape on female trees. The tree has an aromatic fragrance resembling cedar or a cross between pine needles and orange peels. The red sticky sap smells like turpentine.

Elephant tree (Bursera microphylla)

The elephant tree is related to myrrh and frankincense of the Middle East. It has the same sacred and medicinal value to Native Americans as it did to early Arabic and Judaic cultures who also found it economically important as a source of incense and perfume.

Cahuilla Indians believed that the sap had great power. It was always hidden and used by tribal Shamans in curing skin disorders and sexual transmitted diseases. They also used the dried sap as a good luck charm during Indian games.

Elephant tree can be a stunning accent plant and focal point in the garden.

Screwbean mesquite (Prosopis pubescens)

Mesquite (*Prosopis*) is among the toughest and must useful trees for the desert. There are different species; what they all have in common is dark bark and spreading, picturesque branch canopies that cast light, airy shade.

An ordinary sized tree will contain as many as fifty thousand blossoms—a paradise for bees and beekeepers. I had a chance to taste Mesquite honey. It is one of the best—delicious in flavor, pure white in color, and rich in sweetness. One tree can yield more than two pounds of honey.

Honey mesquite (*Prosopis glandulosa*) is deciduous. It grows into a large spreading tree twenty-five feet tall and with a spread of thirty feet. The flowers are sweet smelling and develop into straw-colored leathery pods about five inches long.

It is one of the finest shade trees in the desert. It provides a somewhat dense shade in the summer and allows the sun's ray to penetrate during the colder months.

The seeds feed a variety of desert birds and the thorny foliage provides cover.

It was the most important food source for Native Americans. With its deep roots reaching down to the water table, mesquite produced some food even in the driest years. The fruits ripen in summer and early fall at which time the Native Americans harvested them. They would grind the beans into powder and add some water to make a mush. From this they would bake large cakes which could be stored until they were needed.

Native Americans used all parts of the mesquite. The flowers were collected in spring, roasted, and pressed into a ball for eating or they were used to make a tea. A tea was also made from the leaves; this was supposed to inhibit diarrhea. A mixture of leaves and twigs performed the duty of disinfectant on cuts and minor wounds. Washing the eyes with a rinse made from the pods treated conjunctivitis. The sap was used as an adhesive. The trunk could be hollowed and used as a mortar for grinding. The branches were used to make bows. All woody parts made excellent firewood. Today mesquite charcoal is used for the pleasant flavor it adds to meat.

Screwbean mesquite (*Prosopis pubescens*) is somewhat smaller than the honey mesquite, growing into a fifteen-foot multi-trunk tree with a similar spread. It derives its name from the unusually coiled two-inch long fruits. Its use by Native Americans was much the same as the honey mesquite.

Can you imagine a garden of silver? All gray against the brilliant blue of the desert sky. If so, Smoketree is for you. **Smoketree (*Psorothamnus spinosus, syn., Dalea spinosa*)** is normally found in desert washes. Here their seeds lie dormant, sometimes for years, until life-giving water rushes through, enabling germination.

Smoketree

The elaborate arrangement of slender spiny gray branches gives this tree the appearance of a cloud of smoke. It's a small tree, normally reaching a height of fifteen feet with a width of about ten feet but with summer water can reach a height of as much as thirty feet. A cloud of deep violet-blue flowers embellish the tree and perfume the air in late spring and early summer.

Smoketree can be used as an accent plant in the garden or it can be combined with other gray-leaved plants such as Brittlebush and Desert Lavender. Just be sure to keep it well away from walkways as brushing against it can be a prickly experience.

Smoketree with brittlebush

Desert Shrubs

If trees are the backbone in the landscape, shrubs are its ribs. Shrubs give you privacy in your garden and they provide shelter and food for wildlife.

Wherever I see undeveloped land I notice green shrubs flourishing, even in the middle of summer and in times of drought. Among sere brown grasses and leafless shrubs, the Creosote bush lights up the landscape like a cheerful scarf on a gloomy day.

Creosote bush (*Larrea tridentata*)), also known as greasewood, is the signature plant of the Colorado Desert. It is the 'coolest' plant for the hottest climate.

I'm fascinated by the ways it has successfully met the challenges of desert life by the use of several mechanisms: Its root system infuses the earth around it in a way that enables it to attract every available particle of moisture in its vicinity. It inhibits the growth of

Bur Sage among others. However, after a rainy season a profusion of shallow rooted wild-flowers will crop up around the creosote. But that's the exception. In general, even its own seedlings have a hard time competing for water. To reproduce it rather selfishly lays claim to surrounding ground by sending out new stems from its base, creating an expanding network of roots. As the creosote spreads outward, the inner stems die and the bush expands into larger and larger rings that continues to grow and expand. In other words, it clones itself. The remnants of one plant (clone) have survived for more than 11,000 years, making it one of the oldest individual organisms on earth. In the garden the creosote bush will typically reach a height of nine feet with as wide a spread.

If you watch carefully, you'll notice how the small olive-green leaves turn to avoid the direct rays of the sun. The leaves also have a resinous covering that reflect heat and slow evaporation. This resin makes it taste bad to discourage browsing animals. However, during drought conditions when nothing else is available jackrabbits will eat creosote leaves.

Creosote bush with flowers and seedpods

Moisture in the air releases a strong scent that is "the smell of the desert." Try cupping your hands around the leaves and breathe on them, the moisture of your breath will discharge the aroma.

During most of the year, yellow blossoms sprinkle the foliage followed by fluffy, cotton-like seed pods.

Through the ages, the creosote bush has been the medicine chest for the Cahuilla Indians, functioning much like penicillin. A decoction of leaves was used as an antiseptic on sores and wounds. The Indians bathed in it as an aid for rheumatism. A tea brewed from the leaves was used for treating colds, chest infections, stomach cramps, and runny noses. I have friends who swear by this remedy when they feel a cold coming on. They tell me that the taste is rather unpleasant but can be made palatable with a spoonful of honey or agave nectar.

Creosote was also used for eradicating dandruff, eliminating body odors, inducing vomiting, and remedying constipation. It wasn't just a people medicine; it was also used to treat horses for colds and distemper.

Its resins provided a glue used in arrow making and pottery mending. In Mexico, flower buds are eaten pickled in vinegar.

At present it is used to preserve butter and other edible fats. The leaf residue contains as much protein as alfalfa and can be used in livestock feed.

In the landscape the delicate foliage of Creosote bush is an excellent contrast to the bold forms of cacti and agaves. As an additional benefit, it provides a protected place where wild things can find peace and refuge.

Indigo Bush (*Psorothamnus schottii*) is a relative to the Smoketree but blooms earlier in the season, thus ensuring constant nectar for pollinators.

The new growth of this five feet high, many-branched shrub is bright green, turning gray-green as it matures. The foliage is typically meager which makes the deep purple flowers eye-catching.

I like the combination of the silver look of Indigo bush and Smoketree contrasted with the bright green of the Creosote bush to simulate a desert landscape in the garden.

The Indigo bush was a source of dye for desert dwelling Indians. A tea made from the boiled stems of the bush was used to treat coughs and influenza. Stems were chewed for toothache.

Jojoba (*Simmondsia chinenses*) has many names; it's known as Goatnut, Lemonleaf, Quinine plant, wild hazel, and coffeebush. This three to nine feet tall, gray-green or yellowish spreading shrub is unisex. It has male and female flowers on separate plants. Flowering occurs anytime from December to July. The male flowers are yellow-green and form clusters the size of marbles. The female flowers are solitary. They develop into inch-long, acorn-like fruits with edible seeds. The nuts are noted for their oil content that has been used to replace whale oil in cosmetics and as a precision lubricant. The oil is also used in cooking.

Native Americans considered the nuts a good food source. They ate the nuts raw or made a drink by boiling a meal prepared from roasted nuts and draining off the liquid. Early white settlers ground and mixed the seeds with boiled egg yolks, sugar, and milk for a coffee substitute.

Both domestic and wild animals eat the seeds. Deer and bighorn sheep eat the plant.

Jojoba is tough and undemanding without flashy flowers or unusual foliage. This lack of distinction makes it useful for many landscape situations. Its dense foliage is valuable in creating visual screens and windbreaks. Its lack of thorns makes it a good choice for planting along walks. The run of the mill foliage draws attention to bold, sculptural agaves and cacti.

If you like to attract hummingbirds to your garden, Chuparosa is the shrub to plant. The name comes from the Spanish "chupar," meaning "to suck," referring to its popularity with hummingbirds. Native Americans also sucked on their nectar and the cucumber flavored flowers were eaten by the Papago Indians.

Chuparosa (*Justicia california*) has gray-green branches and leaves that form an open, twiggy shrub about three feet tall and four feet wide. It'll drop its small, heart-shaped leaves during extreme draught or cold but its deep red tubular clusters of flowers appear most of the year.

Chuparosa (*Justicia california*)

Chuparosa flower

Desert plants are tough and well-armed. I approach cautiously with my pruning shears and often come away bloodied from stickers and prickers, thorns and claws. However, there're exceptions.

Desert Lavender (*Hyptis emoryi*) is huggable. I just want to put my arms around it and take pleasure in the softness of its gray leaves covered with fine hairs, and the sweet-smelling fragrance it releases when you brush against it. After rain the lovely smell scents the air.

It has an upright form and makes an excellent informal hedge or privacy screen. It can grow to a height of ten feet with a spread of eight feet.

I love to watch bees visiting the fragrant silvery-blue flowers that bloom throughout the year and I look for birds nesting among the branches.

Bladderpod (*Cleome arborea*) gets its name from its two inch long oval inflated fruits resembling a fat pea pod. Bladderpod has a taste reminiscent of radish; it belongs to the caper family and is a cousin of the plant that produces capers used for seasoning. I like the look of this two to nine foot tall shrub but the foliage is rather rank-smelling when bruised. However, for several months, starting in early spring, clusters of lovely yellow flowers cover the rounded form of Bladderpod, making it an attractive addition to a naturalistic desert landscape.

Apache Plume (*Fallugia paradoxa*) grows to a height of six feet with a four foot width. I like this shrub for a variety of reasons. First of all, it blooms in summer—from May to September—when most desert shrubs are without flowers. Its one and one-half inch white flowers turn into clusters of pink one inch long feathery seed tails that form a fuzzy ball resembling an Apache's headdress. Apache Plume provides both color and texture in your landscape. The dense dark green evergreen foliage is white or reddish on the underside and contrasts with a flaky grayish-white bark.

Is your hair thinning? Some Native Americans used a decoction from the leaves to promote hair growth. It had other uses as well; a powder made from the roots and mixed with similar powders from the tobacco plant was applied to joints as a pain reliever. When the roots were boiled they provided a tonic to treat coughs. The leaves were used for indigestion.

Both livestock and deer have this plant on their menu.

Arrow Weed (*Pluchea sericea*) is a willow-like shrub up to twelve feet tall that likes to have its feet wet. In nature it grows on river bottoms, ditches, and other wet places. It is one of the few shrubs with pink flowers, blooming between March and July. Arrow Weed obtained its name from the use of the straight stems in arrow-making by Native Americans who also used it in construction of their dwellings.

It's rare to see it in a garden setting but I think it would lovely if you happen to have a wet spot or want to create an oasis-like scenery.

Fairy Duster (*Calliandra eriophylla*) provides a spectacular show of pink flowers from February to May, like a misty cloud. It is a rounded shrub with an open growth to three feet and spreading to four feet; it is very drought resistant. When I eliminated my lawn, I planted groups of Fairy Dusters as a substitute. The airy look lends a light texture to the landscape. The flowers attract hummingbirds and rodents eat the seeds.

A close relative is **Baja Fairy Duster (*Calliandra california*)** which blooms most of the year with brilliant red powder-puff like flowers. It grows to a height of about four feet with as wide a spread and makes an excellent informal hedge. It is a native to Baja California and doesn't tolerate temperatures below 25 degrees Fahrenheit or the branch tips will be damaged. However, if you plant it in a protected spot it performs beautifully.

Air currents sing through the slender, pale green, apparently leafless stems of **Mormon Tea (*Ephedra californica*)**. This erect broom-like shrub with jointed branches and pairs of scale-like leaves was useful to Native Americans and to early settlers who brewed a tea that was both a tonic and a beverage. It produced a lift, like coffee and other caffeine drinks. In winter, when other food is scarce, deer and bighorn sheep like to browse the plant.

The three foot high, three foot wide shrub mixes well with leafy desert shrubs such as brittlebush and creosote bush. Or you can use it by itself as an interesting accent plant since it looks quite different from other desert plants.

Flowers, Fillers, and Accent Plants

Trees and shrubs form the framework that defines the space—the skeleton. Now, let's add some flesh to those bones. Flowers, grasses, and accent plants contribute the grace notes that make the space uniquely yours.

Succulents are popular in water wise gardens. They are plants that have the ability to store water in times of plenty in preparation for times of scarcity—like building a nest egg. Any moisture collected is stored within a shiny, waxy, felted, or barked surface to avoid transpiration. Some plants form a large water-storing base while others have reduced surface area of their stems and leaves to cut back evaporation in extreme heat. In the case of cacti, thorns are actually modified leaves.

Cacti are the most widely known of the succulents in the desert and their flowers are spectacular. On immature plants the flowers can be as large as the plant itself.

Cacti have a root system consisting of a shallow, dense network that spreads over a large area, close to the surface of the soil. These fibrous roots enable fast absorption of the lightest rainfall.

California barrel cactus (*Ferocactus cylindraceus*) is an erect, unbranched, barrel-like, ribbed cactus. It is among the largest cacti of the North American deserts. When I look up the mountainside I see plants reaching a height of nine feet with a diameter of eighteen inches.

California barrel cactus is fiercely armed with heavy spines. The yellow to orange bell-shaped flowers are about three inches across and always grow on top of the plant. I've seen them in bloom as early as April and as late as July. Squirrels and birds are attracted to the fleshy and often juicy fruits. Buds, seeds, and flowers are deemed fit for human consumption.

Native Americans boiled young flowers in water to eat like cabbage. They mashed and boiled older flowers for a drink. In times of emergency they pounded the pulp to release its moisture. They used the cactus as a cooking pot by cutting off the top, scooping out the pulp, and heating the chamber with hot stones. Spines were used as awls or needles for sewing and tattooing. In modern times, the pulp of barrel cactus has been used for making a popular cactus candy.

In the garden the solid form of a barrel cactus, or maybe a grouping of three, creates a strong focal point and you can enjoy watching the squirrels and birds feeding on the fruit.

California barrel cactus has an interesting development quirk. It grows faster on the shady side so it always has a definite lean towards the south. If you're lost in the desert without a compass, just look which way the barrel cactus is pointing. At least you won't be walking around in circles. I hope.

Barrel cactus pointing towards the sun

Desert cholla and **Prickly-pear (_Opuntia_)** are abundant in the Colorado Desert. Backlit by the sun chollas glisten in the landscape like splintered glass. And like glass they can be dangerous to the unwary. They have long, thin spines that penetrate clothing and skin and seem to jump at anybody who ventures in their vicinity. They literally get under your skin. What's worse, those spines have little barbs, making it nearly, impossible to get rid of them.

There are several species of cholla. **Teddy-bear cholla (*Cylindropuntia bigelovii*)**, also known as Jumping cholla, is by far the most aggressive. The branch segments detach easily from the plant so that contact with one spine means that the entire segment follows. Branches lying on the ground snag my shoes as I walk by, making me a conspirator, aiding and abetting in the dispersal and reproduction of these fearsome plants.

I shuddered as I watched wood rats collecting a mass of cholla branches to build a formidable fortress for themselves and their young ones but they didn't seem to be bothered by the thicket of spines. I pity the coyote trying to make a meal of those animals. He'll definitely end up with a sore nose and an empty belly.

Some species of cholla develop a wooden trunk as it matures, resembling a small tree. The spiny branches provide a protected nesting site for the cactus wren and other desert birds.

Silver cholla (*Cylindropuntia echinocarpa*), Pencil cholla (*C. ramosissima*), and Buckhorn cholla (*C. acanthocarpa*) all have spines encased in a loose, paper sheath. Pencil and silver cholla have large, yellowish-green flowers streaked with red. Teddy-bear cholla has pale green to lavender flowers. The flowers of Buckhorn are red, yellow, or greenish yellow. And when do they bloom, you may ask. For all of them, the flowering time is sometime between April and June.

Chollas have cylindrical stems, or joints.

Prickly pears, another member of the Opuntia family, have flattened and spine-covered stem pads, which grow on top of one another to form a succulent shrub.

Pancake prickly-pear (*Opuntia chlorotica*) is almost tree-like, growing up to ten feet tall with a stout trunk. The spines are yellow and, on older stems, become dense to generate a hairy look.

Old Man prickly-pear (*Opuntia erinacea*) is barely a foot tall with white to pale-gray wicked spines commonly five inches long or more.

Mojave prickly-pear (*Opuntia phaeacantha*) has stem sections less than six inches across and rarely more than four spines per cluster. The flowers are red and the flesh of the fruit is green. The fleshy pulp of prickly pear fruits is edible either raw or cooked into a jam.

Beavertail cactus (*Opuntia basilaris*) looks relatively harmless but that's an illusion. Its pads are dotted with tiny spines (glochids) that easily get in your skin, causing an irritating itch. These are nearly invisible and hard to remove. I stand in the sunlight to see them and use a pair of tweezers to get them out. I always wear gloves when working in the garden but have to discard my gloves if the glochids get into them. Laundering doesn't help; the glochids are there to stay. If I ever have to prune or transplant a cactus, I use bubble wrap and rolled newspapers to protect myself.

Beavertail cactus has low spreading growth to two to three feet and is seldom more than one foot tall. The stems are blue-green to purplish and the showy magenta flowers make an impressive display for three to four weeks in late spring or early summer.

Native Americans would carefully rub the pads of this plant in sand to remove the glochids; they would pit roast and eat the young fruit. The fleshy pads were cut into strips and added to other food or were dried in the sun and stored, sometimes for years, until needed. The pulp was used as a dressing for injuries to deaden pain. If warts were a problem, they'd rub glochids into them.

Today, I buy jars of stripped and cleaned cactus pads at the supermarket. They are called "nopales" and are delicious in a salad.

One of my friends has planted various Opuntias at the perimeter of her property. It makes an excellent and interesting security fence. Most Opuntia has fragile-looking but spectacular flowers followed by showy yellow or red fruits.

During the hot months you might notice cottony fuzz on some prickly pears. What you're seeing is cochineal—a small scale insect that has a history going back through the ages.

In ancient Mexico, before the time of Christ, the people cultivated these insects that feed exclusively on prickly pear cactus. A female cochineal bug contains carminic acid which produces a brilliant red dye, used by the ancient Mexicans and sold in Aztec marketplaces. This legendary red dye produced the brightest, strongest red ever seen.

In the early 1500s cochineal attracted the attention of the Spanish conquistadors who shipped it to Europe where it created a sensation and became one of the world's most treasured commodities.

When you puncture the insect you'll see a vivid magenta liquid. However, if cochineal is left on the plant it will weaken it and cause yellowing of the pads. I use a stick to scrape off as much as I can, then squirt it with a hose to clean it up.

Prickly pear infested with cochineal

All cacti are succulents but not all succulents are cacti. I used to confuse euphorbia plants with cacti because they have spines on the stem. Then I found out that the way to tell them apart is to look at the spines: euphorbia spines are almost always a pair united at the base, while cacti thorns are never paired. Cacti produce little clusters of white hairs called areoles on the edges or body of the plant. From these distinctive felt-like structures groups of prickles arise. The flowers of cacti are large and showy while euphorbia flowers are tiny and arranged in a complicated, cuplike structure. Most euphorbia species have acrid, milky sap which can irritate skin and cause pain in contact with eyes or open cuts.

Pencil Tree

Pencil tree (*Euphorbia tirucalli*) has found a home in my garden. Its tangle of pencil thick, light green stems with orange tips grabbed hold of my imagination for a narrow bed next to my driveway where it would greet me coming and going. Little did I know how big it would become; in open ground Pencil tree can grow into a thirty foot tall tree. With no supplemental irrigation my little plant has grown into a four foot shrub and, I've noticed, has become a hiding space for a family of California ground squirrels.

In the spirit of disclosure I must tell you that this is not a Colorado Desert native. It's indigenous to Swaziland. However, it has performed so well through heat and cold that I felt it deserved to be included. It is also noninvasive so it presents no threat to native species.

Slipper plant, Candelilla (*Pedilanthus macrocarpus*)

The same goes for another euphorbia which is of Baja origin, the Lady Slipper—so called because its "flower" resembles an old-fashioned pinkish shoe. A friend presented me with a cutting. I stuck the bare stem in the soil and in no time it grew to a height of more than six feet and multiple upright green stems. When it becomes too full, I cut some stems and plant them elsewhere in my garden or I place them in pots to present them as gifts to friends and neighbors. I like their dramatic silhouette against a light wall.

Slipper plant flower

Other succulent plants are the agaves. There are more than three hundred species of agaves ranging in size from minute to gigantic. What they have in common are sword-like leaves and a bold form that contrasts vividly with the fine texture of most desert trees and shrubs.

Cacti and agaves are both New World (the Americas) plants. Their bold and sculptural forms complement each other when used in the garden.

Desert Agave (*Agave deserti*) has a rosette of gray-green, long and pointed leaves with toothed margins, and grows directly on the ground. The plant itself rarely grows taller than one and a half foot with a two foot spread but it forms colonies that may reach ten feet in diameter.

Agaves are also called the century plants. It was believed that the plants lived one hundred years before flowering and then dying. In fact, depending on conditions, agaves can mature anytime between five and fifty years. It then sends up a flower stalk from five feet to fifteen feet tall. The flower is yellow, small, and clustered broadly at the top of the stalk between May to July.

Desert Agave (*Agave deserti*)

    I inherited a trio of Century plants in my garden. They turned out to be *Agave sisalana* which have much larger leaves than the Desert agave and, I found out, can become invasive. When my Century plants began to develop a stalk I couldn't believe how they seemed to shoot up in front of my eyes, growing more than three inches a day. Before dying, they ensured the survival of the species by scattering seeds that germinated with the encouragement of a little water. They also left behind their progeny which I thought was going to overtake my garden. I started to feel like Sleeping Beauty; imprisoned within thorny bushes while waiting for rescue by the handsome prince. In my case I didn't wait for a fairytale prince but hired help to remove the menacing plants while I could still get out of my house. I saved some pups to be planted in pots which would contain them and replaced the original trio with Desert Agave.

    Agave had many uses for the Native Americans. They made rope, bowstrings, and cloth from leaf fibers and used the sharp leaf points as needles. The heart of the plant, when peeled, pulped, and cooked in a fire pit, tastes like sweet potatoes. The young flower stalks were roasted and eaten and so were the flowers. Seeds were ground into flour. Some tribes manufactured an alcoholic drink from the juice of the plant. Tequila is made from Blue Agave which is farmed in the town of Tequila in Mexico. I can think of nothing better than a refreshing Margarita on a hot summer day.

Agave nectar is available in health food stores. I use it as a sweetener; it's sweeter than honey and healthier than sugar.

A number of years ago I planted a **Desert Spoon (*Dasylirion wheeleri*)**, a relative of the agave, in a corner of my planned succulent garden. Its three feet long, one inch wide gray-green slender leaves arc from a central trunk into a rounded shape of three to four feet, showing a graceful symmetry. I find it effective when complemented by fine-textured groundcovers or shrubs. I also like the interesting contrast they make when planted with cacti such as prickly pear or barrel cactus.

Native Americans used the leaves as eating tools. A ragged hem of tan, dry leaves shelters birds, small mammals, and reptiles.

Last summer my Desert Spoon bloomed for the first time. Greenish white, very small flowers clustered in the thousands at the top of a fifteen foot stalk. The male and female flowers are found on different plants and the seeds are dispersed by wind. I only have one plant, sex unknown, so unless there's a mate in the neighborhood I won't have any seedlings.

Desert spoon will grow in light shade but full sunlight encourages the best growth.

Mojave Yucca (*Yucca schidigera*), also known as Spanish dagger, is yet another member of the agave family. This plant can grow to twelve feet with a distinct, often branched, trunk with a two foot flowering stalk appearing in March to June.

Yucca was a useful plant for Native Americans who ate the bitter tasting young flowers. Raw, roasted, or pounded into a meal the fruits supplied sustenance. Native Americans also consumed the seeds, roasted or whole, much like we eat sunflower seeds today, or they ground them into flour. Birds and small mammals are attracted to the fruits and seeds. The leaves provided fibers for rope, sandals, and cloth. Even the roots had a function—pounded in water to produce a lather that would serve as a shampoo and as soap in ritual washing.

Were you to ask what my favorite plant is I'd have a hard time answering. It'd be like asking a mother, "Who's your favorite child." Ocotillo, however, would be high on my list.

Ocotillo is one of the most distinctive plants in the Colorado Desert. Its cluster of sturdy cane-like stems rise fifteen to twenty feet from the desert floor and are topped with scarlet flowers in spring, or any time after it rains. Branches are armed with stiff, straight thorns, remnants of primary leaves, and after rain secondary green leaves appear at the bases of the thorns. These secondary leaves drop when the soil dries, thereby restricting water loss. Chlorophyll in the bark allows the plant to photosynthesize while leafless. Ocotillo belongs in the Ocotillo family (*Fouquieriaceae*).

One ocotillo makes a focal point. It's magical—a living sculpture. A row of ocotillo can be planted as a boundary marker. To achieve a Southwestern look simply stick a bunch of ocotillo stems in the ground around an area you want to fence. With some moisture these branches might root and leaf out to create an amazing spectacle.

Native Americans had a variety of applications for the Ocotillo. They used the stems to construct their dwellings. A decoction of the root functioned as a remedy to treat swellings and fatigue. Capsules and flowers are edible. A beverage can be made by soaking the flowers overnight; as soon as my Ocotillo blooms I'm going can try this. Wax from the stems has been used to dress leather.

Flowers bring a cheery note to the garden. One of my favorite flowers is the daisy. I have fond memories of collecting bunches of daisies as a child. On the rare occasions, when I got out of the city, I'd find them growing wild along the roadside. I pulled the petals, one at a time, "he loves me, he loves me not," before presenting the denuded stems to my mom. Now, I grow daisy-like flowers in my garden.

Angelita Daisy (*Hymenoxys acaulis*) is one of the best perennials for year round color in the Colorado Desert. In spring it blooms profusely and its sunny yellow flowers continue to flaunt their splendor throughout the year. A great choice for tight spaces, this compact plant will form a clump one foot tall and one to two feet wide. Its slender dark green leaves harmonize with the one inch flowers which grow above the foliage on leafless stems.

I like Angelita Daisy as a border plant or as a groundcover next to purple verbena. I also like the way it softens the look in a cactus garden. It will reseed occasionally in landscapes where it finds adequate moisture, but is not invasive.

Chocolate flower (Berlandieri lyrata) entices with the most wonderful chocolate aroma. You might wonder if these daisy-like flowers are edible. They won't harm you, but

Chocolate Flower

their taste doesn't live up to the scent's promise. The flowers close in late afternoon only to open again in the morning. In summer they bloom extravagantly; they also reseed easily. I like to prolong the blooming season by deadheading and enjoy watching the butterflies attracted to the flowers.

Desert Marigold (Baileya multiradiata) is irresistible in my opinion. Do find a spot for it in your garden.

Desert Marigolds bloom almost continually. The yellow daisy-like flowers, cresting one foot stems above a compact mound of gray-green foliage, brighten any landscape. This charming short lived perennial reseeds easily and delights by popping up in the most un-expected places.

If you give Desert marigold a sunny location and a little water (don't overdo the irriga-tion) it rewards you with a glorious display of flowers. Scatter the plants in a naturalistic landscape or tuck them in among other showy perennials such as Penstemon or Globe-mallow. It adds color and softness to a cactus garden. As an added bonus the cut flowers last a long time in bouquets.

Desert Marigold (*Baileya multiradiata*)

A desert garden filled with colorful flowers sounds like an oxymoron. Not so. After winter rains the desert favors with an extravagant wildflower splurge. The desert gardener doesn't have to wait for rains that might not appear for five or ten years but can mimic nature by using irrigation.

Penstemon, a relative to snapdragons, brings color to the landscape and attracts hummingbirds. There are several species of Penstemon: **Bush Penstemon (*Penstemon ambiguous*)** forms a small shrub to about three feet in height and width. The foliage is semi-evergreen and white to pink flowers cover the plant from May to August.

Penstemon with Desert Marigold

Firecracker Penstemon (*Penstemon eatonii*) has dark green, pointed leaves from which two foot tall flower stalks arise. Tube-shaped red flowers open along the stalk from March through June.

Palmer Penstemon (*Penstemon palmeri*) has fragrant puffy pale pink flowers from spring into early summer.

Canyon Penstemon (*Penstemon pseudospectabilis*) has rose-purple flowers that bloom from March to May. The leaves are medium green, arrow-shaped that clasp tightly around the three foot high flower stems.

Thurber Penstemon (*Penstemon thurberi*) is a shrubby perennial about one and a half feet high and one foot wide. Lavender or bluish flowers appear at the ends of the branches from April through June.

Summer evenings, when birds retreat to their roosts, bats flitter across the darkening sky. The rising crescendo of cicadas rubbing their wings in a whining chorus, like the scrape of windshield wipers at high speed, signals the beginning of night. That's when the Sacred Datura opens its large white blossom to brighten the darkness like petite lanterns, and their intoxicating fragrance perfumes the air. I'm careful, though, not to plant it where it'll be a hazard to children and pets. Datura belongs in the nightshade family and all parts of the plant are highly toxic.

It is a powerful hallucinogen that has been used for centuries by Shamans skilled in its preparation. Sacred Datura led them to visions enhancing their special powers.

Sacred Datura (*Datura wrightii*)

In modern times, scientists have discovered that Datura contains a vegetable protein (lectin) known to destroy malignant tumor cells. Lectins are carbohydrate binding proteins highly specific for their sugar moieties. Considered direct predecessors to the immune system, purified lectin is used in blood typing in clinical settings.

Evening primrose

Evening primrose (*oenothera berlandieri*) produce a profusion of rose pink, one and a half inch flowers on stems ten to twelve inches high. Despite its name it blooms in the daytime. Some years ago I planted three of these summer blooming perennials. Before I knew it I had hundreds (if not thousands) of plants all over my garden. They even grew in a patch of dirt into which my washing machine drains. Do you get my drift? They are invasive. I vigorously pull the plants when they have finished blooming and I am rewarded with a second and, at times, a third bloom.

I can't help but admire their tenacity.

Dressing It Up

What's a tuxedo without the bowtie and cummerbund? Or the little black dress without pearls? My favorite accessory in the garden is a vine. There's an old saying "doctors bury their mistakes; architects plant vines." Well, vines do more than cover up—they soften and accentuate. Vines add romance in the garden.

Wild grape (*Vitis girdiana*) closely resembles its cultivated cousin. The purple fruits are delicious eaten right off the vine or you can dry them and use them like raisins. The edible leaves are useful for wrapping other foods for a Greek menu. The raw tendrils make a good and healthy snack. Native Americans were way ahead of the French and made wine from the grapes. They used juice from the leaves to treat 'lust' in women.

Snapdragon vine (*Maurandya antirrhiniflora*) has delicate twining stems with green leaves and small pink to purple snapdragon-like flowers. It blooms from spring to fall and dies back in the winter. I like it close to my house where it has a trellis to climb and I can enjoy its fragile beauty. It also looks terrific in a hanging basket.

Take a hike

Take away only photographs and memories, leave no more than a footprint.

The best way to learn about native plants is to go where they grow. And you don't have to travel far. People are crowding the desert but we are fortunate that the mountains curtail development. There are still open spaces to explore. Put on your comfortable shoes (or hiking boots) and discover the various canyons cutting into the mountains.

Close to downtown Palm Springs is Tahquitz Canyon. I park my car at the rangers' station and proceed by heel-to-toe express. Walking along the trail leading into this canyon, the first thing I notice is tracks. Bighorn sheep and mule deer have taken the same route earlier in the day.

As I continue deeper into Tahquitz Canyon I see a cornucopia of plants; enough to set my head spinning with ideas for my own garden.

Further along, I make another discovery. Nestled between cactus covered hillsides and surrounded by rich vegetation, I encounter a spectacular waterfall—the place where part of the classic movie *Lost Horizons* was filmed.

I see the remnants of Cahuilla occupancy in the form of bedrock mortars ground in the rocks. At one point I notice an ancient rock painting and feel transported back a few thousand years.

Mortars ground in the rock.

Another place to visit is the Indian Canyons. Here, close to the San Andreas Fault line, a ravine separates the San Jacinto Mountains and the Santa Rosa mountains. After entering tribal lands, the first canyon I reach is Andreas Canyon.

As I cross the threshold to the canyon, I am overwhelmed by the magnificent rock formations and the diversity of plant life.

Chuckwallas and a multitude of other lizards keep me company as I explore the land-scape.

From Andreas Canyon I follow a path to the neighboring Murray Canyon, which has different vegetation with more ideas for my own landscape. I complete the circle and am back at my car.

Then, I continue my trek across ancestral Cahuilla land where scattered rocks nestle amid a variety of desert plants. The road ends at a Cahuilla Trading Post. I've reached Palm Canyon.

I enjoy a cool drink at one of the tables there while looking down to the largest palm oasis in the world, with more than a thousand California fan palms.

This deserves a closer look. I finish my drink and walk down a steep trail to the bottom of the ravine. Here I see cottonwoods, sycamores, and willows growing along shallow streams gurgling like a happy child.

Nothing in the desert is obvious; the desert is reluctant to reveal its secrets. Looking up at the mountains they give the impression of being devoid of vegetation. However, a careful look exposes a treasure of plant life in its desert camouflage.

The most northern part of the Colorado Desert is at Joshua Tree National Park, which borders the Mojave Desert. I like to go at different times of the year to observe the variety of the seasons. Visit in spring to watch an abundance of Chuparosa in full bloom with a plethora of hummingbirds sucking their juice. Come back on a winter day when snow falls like feathers, garnishing Joshua trees in a diaphanous veil.

I prefer to start at the northern entrance from Highway 62. The first part of the trip takes me through the southern part of the Mojave Desert where I drive through a forest of Joshua trees, their contorted forms like dancers frozen in time.

As I drive south through striking fields of boulders, the Joshua tree forest gives way to impenetrable thickets of cacti. This is a transition zone, the gateway to the Colorado Desert.

I continue on my way and the vegetation changes to a preponderance of Ocotillo, their thorny stalks reaching for the sky.

Deeper into the park I notice Coyote melon racing along the ground as if late for an appointment.

Coyote melon

A large lizard hurries across the sand to seek shelter from the midday sun.

Cheese bush (*Hymenoa salsola*)

An abundance of Cheese bushes are greening out after a brief rain, making a nice contrast to the darker green Creosote bush.

I reach Cottonwood Springs where for centuries the Cahuilla Indians had gathered for seasonal hunting and meetings. Then, with the discovery of gold, it became a center of activity during the mining years of 1870-1910. Here, I stop at the rangers' station for a picnic in the shade of California fan palms before leaving the park and getting on Interstate 10 south of Indio.

Has your curiosity been piqued? Do you want to explore more of the Colorado Desert? I can suggest a visit to the western border of the Colorado Desert, the desert section of Anza-Borrego State Park. For a look at sand dunes, go south to the Algodones Dunes near the Mexican border or make an appointment at the Coachella Valley Preserve for permission to take a tour of the sand dunes in Palm Desert.

Finally, a few last words. The plants described and depicted in this book represent only a fraction of the many plants native to the Colorado Desert. My intention has been

to suggest possibilities for incorporating native plants in your own landscape and to inspire gardeners and landscape designers to explore and expand on them. Some might choose to plant only native plants. Others might want to grow a wider variety of low water-use plants—a mixture of natives and plants from other arid climates.

As the population grows, the least any of us can do is to be mindful of our individual and collective impact on natural resources—clean air, clean water, energy, open space, and biodiversity—and to accept personal responsibility for our actions.

Plant Index

Acknowledgments

I owe a debt of gratitude to my writers' group, Fran and Harold Kaplan, Steve Scott, Patty Willingham, and Jim Duggins. Their unfailing encouragement, gentle critique, and pertinent questions helped shape this book.

And a multitude of extra thanks to Jim Duggins for taking on the enormous task of editing the final draft.

Jennifer Purcell willingly shared her extensive knowledge of the Colorado Desert and all its inhabitants. Thank you, Jennifer, for reading through my first draft and preventing me from giving out misinformation.

I want to thank my dear friend, Anita Kornfeld, for supporting my writing endeavors through the years.

Last but not least, my thanks to the staff and volunteers at The Living Desert for the wonderful work you do in conservation, preservation, and education about our wonderful desert and the deserts of the world.

Fritzie von Jessen